ENCYCLOPEDIA OF MAMMALS

VOLUME 10
Mol–Opo

MARSHALL CAVENDISH

NEW YORK • LONDON • TORONTO • SYDNEY

MOLES

Liz Bomford/Ardea

GROUND BURROWERS

WHILE OTHER MAMMALS EVOLVED INTO A WEALTH OF RUNNERS, CLIMBERS, FLIERS, AND SWIMMERS, MOST MOLES SIMPLY HEADED FOR THE GROUND, DEVELOPING IN THE DARKNESS BENEATH OUR FEET

Moles, desmans, and golden moles have altered less dramatically than many mammals over the course of time. When dinosaurs stalked the earth 150 million years ago, small, furry creatures lived alongside them. Dental evidence from these creatures suggests that they lived on insects and other small invertebrates, and it was from such relatively humble beginnings that the abundance of mammal species that exist today evolved.

Features of some of the earliest mammals, such as small body size, a long, pointed snout, and a coat of short fur, are the same features that have been retained by the modern-day insectivores—an order including moles, shrew-moles, desmans, and golden moles along with hedgehogs, shrews, and tenrecs.

Insectivores include some of the most primitive of placental mammals, but they are today a highly successful group with over 350 species, occurring on every continent except Australia and Antarctica.

1381

The golden mole's tough nose-pad comes into service during digging operations (below).

Anthony Bannister/NHPA

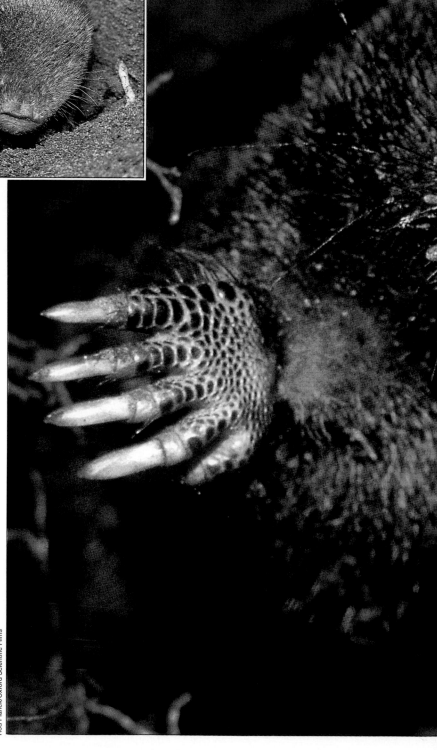

Rod Planck/Oxford Scientific Films

They have evolved to exploit a broad range of land and semiaquatic habitats, and their sheer diversity almost defies classification, so that there is still some uncertainty over just which mammals should be included among the Insectivore order.

Nevertheless, most species display certain unifying features. They are small, active insect-feeders, although they will feed on a variety of invertebrates along with the occasional small vertebrate and plant material when the opportunity presents itself. The manner of movement of insectivores is restricted by their short limbs—walking is in a plantigrade style, with heels and toes both firmly on the ground. These mammals have tiny, sometimes invisible ears and eyes; in the case of the golden moles, sight has been entirely lost.

EUROPEAN DOWN UNDER

The European mole is a fairly typical member of the Talpidae family of "true" moles or talpids, all of which are found in the Northern Hemisphere. It is also probably the best studied of all talpids. A restless creature, this mole hunts feverishly at roughly four-hour intervals throughout the day and night.

The European mole is thought to have originated as a woodland species, which later colonized the more dense and well-drained soil of fields and other open areas. It lives underground and is well suited to burrowing. The tiny eyes are almost hidden by fur, so the mole relies upon smell and hearing to locate prey and avoid danger. The limbs are modified for shifting as much soil as possible, the spadelike forepaws being used for digging. The burrow system often comprises both shallow, surface runs, where

EVOLUTION

The members of the six families within the Insectivore order share skull and dental features, which suggest that they are all descended from a common ancestor. All eat invertebrates, particularly insects, and have a set of forty-four teeth, the fullest set generally found in placental mammals. This continuous row of teeth typically consists of three incisors, one canine, four premolars, and three molars in each half jaw.

Moles evolved from shrewlike insectivore ancestors from the Eocene epoch (55–38 million years ago). A split at around this time led to the development of the subfamily Desmaninae (desmans) in the Old World, and the subfamily Proscalopinae, from which evolved the family Talpidae, in the New World. Moles of the genus *Talpa* are among the most highly specialized moles, while the most primitive living mole is the Chinese shrew-mole from southern China. The evolutionary origin of the American star-nosed mole remains obscure.

the mole may be only a hand's width below the soil surface, and a system of more permanent tunnels at deeper levels.

As in many other mole species, the European species is solitary and active mostly at night. It feeds mainly on earthworms; these usually prove to be an easy meal, since they literally drop in on the mole's tunnels as they pass through the soil.

MOLES WITH A DIFFERENCE

Desmans are rather atypical members of the family Talpidae. There are only two species: the Pyrenean desman and the Russian desman. The former species is confined to fast-flowing streams of the Pyrenees mountain range and parts of northern Iberia, while the Russian desman is found in the slower-moving waters of lakes and ponds of the western and central former USSR. Desmans feed on aquatic insects, which they catch by diving to the bottom of shallow watercourses. Consequently they are well suited to a semiaquatic lifestyle, having a streamlined body with waterproof fur, powerful webbed hind feet, and a long, broad tail that acts as a rudder. The long, proboscislike snout is used to probe beneath small rocks and other streambed debris to seek out their prey.

The star-nosed mole digs deep tunnels by rivers or lakes; many of these lead directly to the water.

The golden moles of southern and central Africa, family Chrysochloridae (cry-so-CLORE-i-die), resemble more closely the European mole. They, too, are adapted for a subterranean way of life, with a robust, compact body, short limbs, and formidably clawed forepaws. The tiny eyes are useless, remaining closed from birth and later becoming covered

with hairy skin. The senses of touch and smell are consequently important to these creatures. For protection against sand and soil, the ear openings are covered by fur and the nostrils are capped by a leathery pad on the snout. Golden moles are heavily dependent on thrusts of the powerful head and shoulders to bulldoze soil from their path.

Like moles, golden moles have extensive burrow systems, and for most golden mole species, the main food items are the earthworms and other invertebrates, which they happen upon in their tunnel networks. However, certain desert-dwelling species such as Grant's golden mole do not construct permanent tunnel systems, but simply push or "swim" their way through the loose, topmost layer of the sand dunes, locating prey by touch and sound. Desert golden moles occasionally emerge to hunt over the surface for insects and legless lizards. Their sensitive ears can detect the faintest of vibrations, and these species also have a good sense of orientation; they are able, for example, to reconstruct burrow systems that have been damaged by flooding.

Golden moles spend more time on burrowing than on any other single activity. It has been estimated that some species devote up to 75 percent of their active time tunneling busily through the sand and soil. The size and style of burrow varies between species and also depends upon the type of habitat that the species occupies. ■

Color illustrations Kim Thompson. B/W Ruth Grewcock

THE MOLES' FAMILY TREE

The family tree shows the relationship between moles, shrew-moles, desmans, golden moles, and other members of the order Insectivora, which originated some 135 million years ago. This single group is subdivided into six families— the Solenodontidae (solenodons), Tenrecidae (tenrecs), Chrysochloridae (golden moles), Erinacidae (hedgehogs and moonrats), Talpidae (moles, shrew-moles, and desmans), and Soricidae (shrews).

GOLDEN MOLES
Chrysochloridae
(cry-so-CLORE-i-die)

The eighteen species of golden mole inhabit dry habitats south of the Sahara. In spite of their name, not all golden moles are golden in color—the Cape golden mole, for example, is dark brown. However, the coats of most species have a glossy sheen.

TENRECS

CONVERGENT MOLES

Convergent evolution is the process in which animals that are not closely related have adapted in similar ways to a specific habitat or way of life. Golden moles are similar to the marsupial mole of Australia, despite the fact that these two groups have evolved separately for 70 million years. In fact, golden moles are more like the marsupial mole than true moles, to which they are more closely related. Both the marsupial mole and golden moles are blind, whereas true moles can see—barely. The marsupial mole and golden moles also share golden brown fur, and both have a leathery nose-pad that is used to shunt soil.

SUBORDER
TENRECOMOR

ALL INSECTIVORES

EUROPEAN MOLE

Talpa europaea
(TAL-pah yoo-ro-PAY-ah)

The twenty-five species of mole live mainly in the ground under forests, grasslands, and heaths across most of Europe, Asia, and North America. The European mole itself is found from Britain east across Europe, roughly to the Ural Mountains, wherever the soil is deep enough for its tunnel networks. Moles thrive in cultivated farmland—regrettably for the farmers.

DESMANS

Galemys, Desmana
(GAL-em-is, des-MAH-nah)

The two species of desman have webbed toes, waterproof fur, a long, broad tail, and long, powerful legs and feet in relation to their body size. They occur in Europe and Asia—the Pyrenean desman in fast-flowing mountain streams in the Pyrenees, and the Russian desman along low-lying oxbow lakes and swampy rivers in the former USSR.

SUBORDER
RICOMORPHA

SUBORDER
RINACEOMORPHA

SOLENODON

SHREWS

HEDGEHOG

MOONRATS

1385

ANATOMY:
THE EUROPEAN MOL

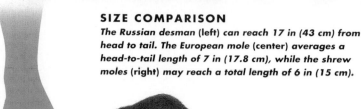

SIZE COMPARISON

The Russian desman (left) can reach 17 in (43 cm) from head to tail. The European mole (center) averages a head-to-tail length of 7 in (17.8 cm), while the shrew moles (right) may reach a total length of 6 in (15 cm).

THE EARS

have evolved without pinnae (external flaps) in order to minimize obstruction in the tunnel network. They are, however, fully functional.

THE EYES

are tiny and sunk deep into the fur. They enable the mole to distinguish between light and dark but are not much use for anything else.

THE SNOUT

is tipped with a set of several thousand touch-sensitive structures known as Eimer's organs. These structures, which are also a feature of desmans (see below), allow the animal to assess minute surface details of objects. Talpid moles have sensory hairs on and under the chin, on the muzzle, and in tufts behind the ears.

STAR-NOSED MOLE

A ring of 22 pink, fleshy tentacles form a star at the tip of the muzzle. This highly sensitive organ helps the animal to locate prey when hunting.

PYRENEAN DESMAN

The nostrils lie at the tip of a long snout extension. The tip is so sensitive that it can detect fissures as small as 0.0024 in (0.06 mm) deep and wide.

THE FOREPAWS

are formed in such a way that the palms face to the outside—ready to dig at a moment's notice.

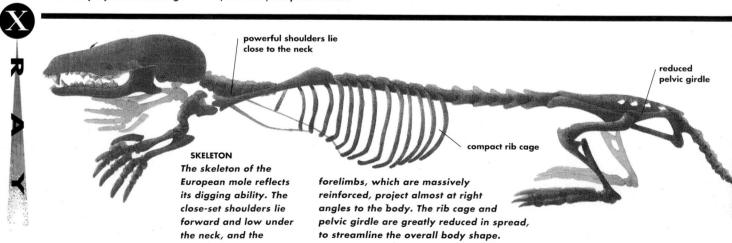

X
R
A
Y

powerful shoulders lie close to the neck

reduced pelvic girdle

compact rib cage

SKELETON

The skeleton of the European mole reflects its digging ability. The close-set shoulders lie forward and low under the neck, and the forelimbs, which are massively reinforced, project almost at right angles to the body. The rib cage and pelvic girdle are greatly reduced in spread, to streamline the overall body shape.

X-ray illustrations Elisabeth Smith

FOREPAWS

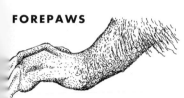

HIND FEET

THE DESMAN'S FEET
In these semiaquatic species, the hind paws are webbed and have fringes of stiff bristles, to make them efficient paddles. The forepaws are semiwebbed and have similar bristles.

THE PELT
is superbly adapted to the mole's lifestyle. Dense and velvety, it lies readily in any direction; this enables the mole to turn and reverse easily within a tunnel. The hairs are some 0.25 in (6.4 mm) long in summer, 0.35 in (8.9 mm) in winter, and are molted at least twice a year.

THE HIND FEET
are more delicate than the forepaws, but are similarly equipped with five stout claws. The hind feet help to brace the mole against tunnel walls while it digs with its forepaws.

FACT FILE:

THE EUROPEAN MOLE

CLASSIFICATION

FAMILY: TALPIDAE

GENUS: *TALPA*

SIZE

HEAD–BODY LENGTH: 4.3–6.7 IN (11–17 CM)

TAIL LENGTH: 0.8–1.3 IN (2–3.3 CM)

WEIGHT: 2.1–4.2 OZ (59.5–119 G)

WEIGHT AT BIRTH: 0.1–0.14 OZ (2.8–4 G)

COLORATION

THE VELVETY COAT IS BLACK, AND SOMETIMES SHOWS A SILVERY LUSTER

THE FUR OF THE UNDERSIDES IS PALER

FEATURES

CYLINDRICAL BODY

NO EXTERNAL EARS

LARGE, PINK FOREPAWS

DENSE, VELVETY COAT

TINY EYES

SHORT, CLUB-SHAPED TAIL

HAIRLESS, FLESHY, PINK SNOUT

BROAD, SPADELIKE FORELIMBS, DEVELOPED AS POWERFUL DIGGING AIDS; ATTACHED TO MUSCULAR SHOULDERS AND A DEEP CHEST BONE

SHORT, STURDY HIND LIMBS

THE TAIL
is short, to suit the mole's burrowing habit, and is usually held erect. It is equipped with sensory bristles.

---

scapula (shoulder blade)

tibia and fibula (forearm) fused at base

paw

fossorial claw

humerus

FOREQUARTERS
Whereas the shoulder blades are slimmed down, the humerus (upper arm) on each forelimb is enormous, forming a broad anchorage for the digging muscles. A sickle-shaped bone known as the fossorial claw helps to support the broad forepaws.

TEETH
The crowns of the cheek teeth have W-shaped cusps for crushing insects.

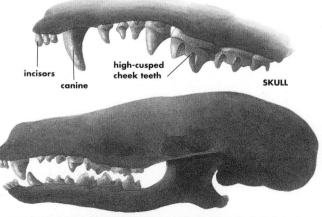

incisors

canine

high-cusped cheek teeth

SKULL

Color illustrations Steve Kingston

EARTH MOVERS

MOLES WILL MAKE THEIR HOME, WHEREVER THERE ARE PLENTY OF INVERTEBRATES TO EAT. FOR SOME SPECIES THIS MEANS A LIFE SPENT TUNNELING THROUGH SOIL; OTHERS HAVE TAKEN TO WATER

D igging for a living is a specialized habit to which moles are superbly adapted. They need to be: For a mole to dig a yard of tunnel requires up to 4,000 times as much energy as it does for the animal to walk the same distance on the soil surface. Most of this energy is spent shunting piles of loose soil out of the tunnel system, rather than in the actual process of digging.

Whereas true moles are generally found in soil types that will support fixed tunnels, this is not true of all moles. Certain species of golden mole, for example the Namib golden mole, live in unstable soils. As this mole searches for its prey of lizards and invertebrates by squirming through the hot, shifting sands of the Namib Desert, any sand that it moves is instantly replaced. As a result, permanent tunnels and molehills are rarely found, and then only in areas of damp, compacted ground. In loose sand, the golden mole's progress shows up as a network of sandy ridges where the mole has passed just below the surface. Similarly, Grant's golden mole of the southwest Cape, South Africa, quite literally swims through the sand. This species has earned the nickname of "sand fish."

USING THEIR HEADS

A golden mole digs with its head and limbs; the muscular shoulders and head buttress the soil, which is compacted and shunted by the leathery snout. The forelimbs are then used to scrabble away at the soil. These animals are phenomenally strong: Studies in captivity show that a golden mole can move an object equal to 150 times its own weight.

Talpid moles do not actively use their heads in the digging process, but paddle their limbs in the horizontal plane—rather like a swimmer doing the breaststroke. They dig two types of burrow—shallow surface tunnels, which appear as raised dikes, and deeper runs. Shallow tunnels are particularly common in freshly cultivated fields, in areas of light, sandy soil, and in shallow soils where prey is concentrated close to the surface. Deeper tunnels are found particularly where the soil layer is thick, or under dry conditions when earthworms, the moles' staple prey, have migrated deeper into the soil.

Usually, a mole digs using just one forelimb at a time with the body braced firmly against the tunnel wall by the outstretched hind legs and the free forelimb. The mole shears soil from the working face of the tunnel, pushing it back and upward with the digging forelimb. After two or three strokes the roles of the two forelimbs are reversed. As the mole edges forward through the debris, its body shapes and smooths the tunnel. At intervals, the mole scoops up loose soil and shunts it to the nearest exit shaft, thrusting it onto the surface to add to a molehill.

The bizarre star-nosed mole of North America uses the fleshy tentacles on its snout to detect prey (above).

Paulo de Oliveira/Planet Earth Pictures

Michael Habicht/Oxford Scientific Films

SHREW-MOLES

Of all insectivores, moles are probably the most closely related to shrews, and today the lifestyles of the American and Asiatic shrew-moles bear resemblances to both animals. For example, shrew-moles forage above ground, like shrews, but they also dig shallow burrows.

Shrew-moles are among the smallest members of the mole family. As the name implies, these mammals are shrewlike in appearance and have long tails. Their snouts are long and scaly, and they have conspicuous external ears. The hands are small and not modified for burrowing, and the claws are curved and weak.

There are thought to be three species of Chinese shrew-mole—one of which is the Asiatic shrew-mole of mountain ranges in Szechuan and Yunnan in China and of northern Burma. There is a single species of American shrew-mole, found from British Columbia to central California. It is the smallest of the American moles, with a total length of 4–5 in (10–12.7 cm). The closest relatives to this species are the two species of shrew-mole found in Japan.

Tunnel networks may extend for several hundred yards, and lie between 2–60 in (5–152 cm) below the soil surface.

WATER-DWELLING MOLES

Desmans spend much of their lives swimming. They occasionally forage along the banks of streams for earthworms and beetles, but generally survive on a diet of aquatic insects such as stone fly, mayfly, and caddis fly larvae. They hunt after dark, when their prey is most active. Moles can also swim if they have to; their fur is relatively waterproof and traps large amounts of air, providing buoyancy.

Like the desmans, the star-nosed mole of North America lives a semiaquatic existence—spending time both underground and underwater, and catching prey in both habitats. Often, these curious creatures dig their tunnels close to marshy areas and the exits often lead directly into open water. Star-nosed moles have broader feet than other moles and the strong tail acts as a rudder, helping to steer the animal when swimming. ■

Moles rarely have to leave their tunnels; almost all their needs are catered for below ground.

HABITATS

Of the two mole families, the Talpidae—the moles, shrew-moles, and desmans—have a much wider world distribution than the golden moles. Whereas the Talpidae are spread throughout Europe, Asia, and North America, the golden moles are restricted to sub-Saharan Africa.

Golden moles originated in Africa, probably from a tenreclike ancestor, and have never managed to expand beyond this dry continent. They are confined to areas south of the equator. Golden moles have changed little over time; fossils have been found from 27 million years ago in Kenya, and

---

MOLEHILLS CAN BE MISTAKEN FOR NEST HILLS OF THE YELLOW ANT, BUT THESE ARE LARGER AND MORE STEEPLY SIDED

---

over two million years ago in South Africa. They occur in a wide range of dry habitats, from scrub and swamp edges to dry forests. Many of the species are poorly known and the classification of the group remains provisional.

FOOD-BASED TERRITORIES

Adapted for a digging lifestyle underground, moles can make their home anywhere where the soil is deep enough to support both a tunnel network and sufficient prey animals. If the soil is waterlogged or subject to permafrost, this will limit the moles' distribution. Suitable habitats differ greatly in the

DISTRIBUTION

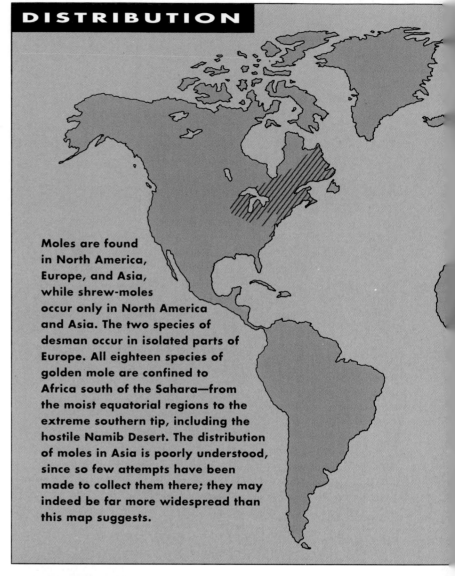

Moles are found in North America, Europe, and Asia, while shrew-moles occur only in North America and Asia. The two species of desman occur in isolated parts of Europe. All eighteen species of golden mole are confined to Africa south of the Sahara—from the moist equatorial regions to the extreme southern tip, including the hostile Namib Desert. The distribution of moles in Asia is poorly understood, since so few attempts have been made to collect them there; they may indeed be far more widespread than this map suggests.

John Hartley/NHPA

The Russian desman lives in burrows or natural hollows beside slow-moving rivers and lakes (left).

amount of food that they can supply, and typically include deciduous woodlands and permanent pastures at one extreme to coniferous forests and near-barren sand dunes at the other. Moles living in habitats with high prey densities—in the order of 0.7–0.8 oz of invertebrates per square foot (200–250 g per square meter) occupy small ranges of 3,228–4,304 square feet (300–400 square meters). In contrast to this, some individuals have been found living in sand dunes where prey is a hundred times more scarce. In this case individual moles had territories a dozen times larger, at more than 1.24 acres (5,000 square meters) in area.

Although moles are rarely seen, every proud gardener whose lawn has been turned overnight into a mountain range will know that they betray their presence in grand style. Molehills lack any

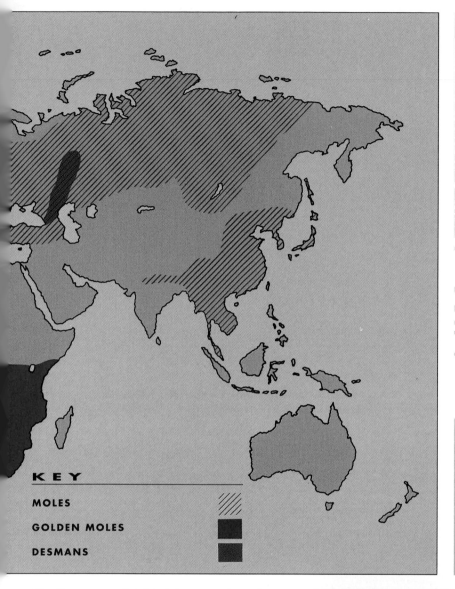

KEY

MOLES

GOLDEN MOLES

DESMANS

KEY FACTS

● Russian desmans face competition from introduced coypus and muskrats in their native habitats, in addition to the drainage of wetlands. Furthermore, particularly heavy frosts may trap desmans beneath the ice.

● The central Pyrenean subspecies of desman is extinct, probably as a result of competition with, or direct predation by, the introduced American mink.

● The giant golden mole of South Africa occurs locally in remnants of forests and in open grasslands. Such habitats are rapidly being converted into grazing and arable pasture.

● Pyrenean desmans are confined to small, fast-flowing watercourses; they rely particularly on the smallest mountain streams bordered by deciduous vegetation, which casts only limited shadows onto the water surface, and allows enough light for both the desman and its prey to survive. In many parts of its range, reforestation with fast-growing coniferous trees has caused dense shade and soil acidification, driving the desmans away.

The European mole (right) *has a penchant for pastures, which are rich in earthworms.*

kind of entrance hole, as they are merely the spoil heaps ejected by the animals in the construction of their tunnel networks. In due course, vegetation, the wind, and the rain leave their mark upon the mounds of loose, rich soil, softening them gradually into the contours of the terrain.

The layout of a tunnel system depends on the soil type, but typically consists of a horizontal network roughly 3–8 in (8–20 cm) beneath the surface, with another horizontal network some 12 in (30 cm) below this. The two networks are linked by a series of shafts. From the lower network, irregular, blind shafts may penetrate to depths of 47 in (119 cm).

Moles do not dig new tunnels every time they go in search of food. Rather, they repeatedly use a series of tunnels over a long period of time for feeding, and several generations of moles may use the

Liz Bomford/Ardea

same series of tunnels, particularly if there is a rich and dependable supply of food, such as is found beneath old pastureland.

DENIZENS OF STREAM AND LAKE

The two species of desman inhabit very different watery homes. The smaller Pyrenean desman, weighing a mere 2 oz (56.7 g), lives in the Pyrenees and parts of northern Iberia, along rushing mountain streams that are well oxygenated and contain high levels of nutrients. This combination supports plenty of aquatic insect prey. The desman may nest in natural hollows among roots; usually, however, it excavates a tunnel with an underwater entrance and an uphill slope to a snug, grass-lined chamber. Highly territorial, a pair of Pyrenean desmans will stoutly defend stretches of stream up to 650–1,300 ft (198–396 m) long against intruders. Within this zone, however, the male and female lead mainly solitary lives.

The Russian desman is a bulky, rat-sized creature by comparison. It lives along slow-flowing or even stagnant watercourses, such as ponds, canals, and lakes. The fossil record for this species suggests that at one time it was distributed right across Europe, from southern Britain in the west to the Caspian Sea in the east. It has become progressively

M. Walker/Frank Lane Picture Agency

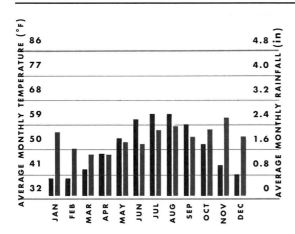

TEMPERATURE AND RAINFALL

■ **TEMPERATURE**

■ **RAINFALL**

The southeast coast is one of England's sunniest regions. It receives less rainfall than the north and west. However, the windchill factor can be severe in winter, as the airstreams blow practically unimpeded from as far afield as the Urals in Russia.

more restricted in range, mainly to large river basins in parts of the former USSR.

The Russian desman is an enthusiastic digger, and will often make its nest deep within the root systems of bankside plants. The nest has two or three entrances, all of which lie well below the water level, ensuring safe and easy access even in winter. The entrances rise to the nest chamber, which is lined with moss and leaves and lies very close to the soil surface. In this way, the chamber is naturally ventilated from above. ■

FOCUS ON

THE SOUTH DOWNS

The chalky South Downs in Sussex and Hampshire, England, are broken into five main blocks by four rivers—the Cuckmere, Ouse, Adur, and Arun—which drain southward over the chalk scarp to the coast. While large parts of the eastern end of the downs are short-tu grasslands, the western hills support beechwoods and, more recently introduced conifer plantations. Dry valleys are a common feature; these are old river valleys that no longer contain rivers or streams a the level of the water table has dropped within the soil.

The close-cropped turf of these southern chalk downs are among richest botanical habitats in Europe: Over twenty species of flowerin plant may be found on an area of turf 12 in (30 cm) square. Over th last few decades, however, much of the downs has been reseeded to create better quality grazing for sheep, and large areas have been turned over to arable land. Hawthorn scrub has invaded many forme pastures; its spread has been exacerbated by the decline of rabbits, which used to provide a natural control on the vegetation. In additio chalklands have succumbed to the general "tidying up" of Britain's countryside, particularly hedge removal.

Chalky soils are favored by moles, being firm and free draining, and permit these burrowers to dig an extended network of permane or semipermanent tunnels.

NEIGHBORS

Chalk grasslands support a particularly rich and diverse flora, which attracts insects, small mammals, and their predators. The bird life includes seasonal migrants from overseas.

BARN OWL

This pale owl hunts over open country in the twilight and night. It preys on small rodents, birds, and insects.

GRASS SNAKE

This nonvenomous snake, with its pale yellow collar, feeds on frogs and is often found in damp locations.

Neighbor illustrations Joanne Cowne, except barn owl by Kim Thompson and rabbit by Chris Christoforou

SOUTH DOWNS

The chalky hills that form the South Downs rise to a modest 850 ft (259 m) above sea level and stretch for 56 miles (90 km) along the south coast of England, from Beachy Head in East Sussex through West Sussex to the border with Hampshire in the west.

SOUTH DOWNS

Inset photograph ZEFA

RABBIT

Introduced to Britain by the Normans, the adaptable rabbit lives colonially in a range of habitats.

SKYLARK

Generally heard before it is seen, the skylark is famous for its twittering song given from high in the sky.

COMMON FROG

Found in damp, shady areas, this frog hibernates in mud at the bottom of ponds during the winter.

HEDGEHOG

Hedgehogs feed mainly on earthworms, but also eat beetles, slugs, millipedes, larvae, seeds, and berries.

PAINTED LADY BUTTERFLY

This common butterfly is a noted migratory species. It has a distinctively fast and erratic flight pattern.

BURROWING

Most moles spend almost their entire lives below ground. Radio-tracking studies of the European mole show that, although neighboring moles inhabit their own tunnel systems, there is some overlap between territories. Moles seem to be fully aware of the presence of their neighbors; in any given activity period, they will forage well away from each other in parts of their territories that are not next to each other.

If a mole disappears from its territory—if it dies or is trapped, for example—neighboring moles are quick to realize this, and will invade and use the existing tunnels, sometimes within hours of their vacancy. With or without such annexes, mole territories may cover a substantial area; in one notable example, the two halves of a mole's territory were found to be connected by a single tunnel running under the two-lane main road between Peterhead and Aberdeen, in northeast Scotland. The resident mole would have had to shunt soil and debris along the entire length of the link tunnel.

> A MALE MOLE MAY INCREASE HIS HOME RANGE TO THREE TIMES ITS NORMAL AREA DURING THE BREEDING SEASON

Within the burrow network, moles generally construct one or more nest chambers. Each of these spherical chambers is packed with a ball of shredded plant material, which the mole obtains either by pulling plants down into the tunnel by their roots, or by collecting plant material from around the burrow entrances. Although dry grass and leaves are the most common nest materials, other items used have included newspaper, scraps of plastic, and crisp wrappers. These nests are used for sleeping or, in the case of the females, for raising young.

FORTRESSES

Although most molehills are small and contain no internal structure, at certain times European moles will heap up mounds of soil up to 1,650 lb (750 kg) in weight. Both male and female moles expend much energy in the construction of these giant molehills, known as fortresses, which have a range of uses and may stand 3 ft (a meter) high. Fortresses are used most often between late autumn and spring; they contain one or two nest chambers and a network of tunnels, including, in some cases, a blind tunnel leading to drinking water. These hills also serve as a food cache where the moles store earthworms for consumption during winter.

Fortresses are most commonly found in areas with a high water table, which are prone to flooding. As the waters rise, the moles can take refuge in the tunnels of the fortress, which are high enough above ground level. Another situation in which fortresses are common is where soils are thin, for example in the Brecklands in the east of England. Here a nest built in a fortress will offer a more stable environment than will a nest close to the surface of a layer of thin soil. Ideally, a mole seeks to construct its nest deep within the soil, both to avoid detection by predators and to avoid the worst extremes of sudden temperature changes.

The different species of golden mole use a variety of burrowing styles. Stuhlmann's golden mole, in

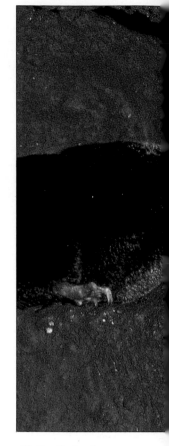

Typically intolerant, a European mole evicts an intruder with a bout of scratching and biting (above). Confrontations are rare, and seldom result in serious injury.

GOLDEN MOLE BURROWS

B/W illustration Ruth Grewcock

Hottentot golden moles live at fairly high densities wherever food is plentiful. But in sites where prey is harder to come by, they dig and defend vast burrow systems, which may extend to three feet (a meter) in depth and contain as much as 820 ft (250 m) of tunnels. The burrows spread laterally close to the surface, and incorporate a few deep, spiraling bolt holes down which the moles scurry when alarmed. These bolt holes may be modified to accommodate nursery and sleeping chambers, which are lined for comfort with grassy vegetation.

MOLE HOLES AN
The European mole's
include exit shafts, by
waste soil is expelled

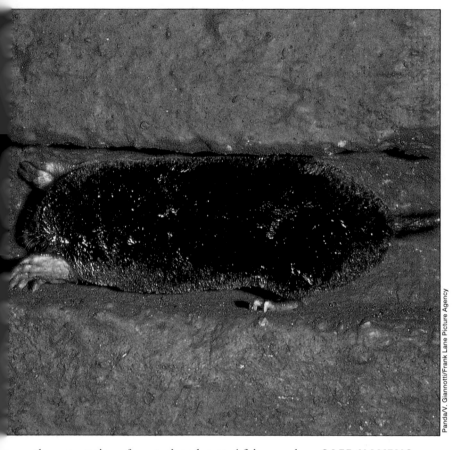

Panda/V. Giannotti/Frank Lane Picture Agency

ⓘSIGHT

BULLDOZING

As there is no space for a mole to compress waste soil into tunnel walls, surplus soil must be moved to the surface. As the mole digs, loose soil is thrown back and down the tunnel by the single digging forepaw and the scrabbling hind paws. Once a heap of soil has built up, the mole turns within the tunnel—sometimes by somersaulting. It then pushes the soil back down the tunnel, away from the freshly dug area, using alternate thrusts of the forepaws. The mole puts all its energy into this Herculean effort, with its paws held diagonally to the body in the manner of a bulldozer's blade. It thrusts the soil up a previously excavated sloping side shaft off the main shaft, and out onto the surface to add to a molehill. The mole will dig new side shafts when there is too great a distance to push earth back to the original lateral shafts. This results in a line of molehills charting the animal's passage.

Color illustration Gareth Llewhellin/Wildlife Art Agency

the mountains of central and east Africa, and Hottentot's golden mole of southern Africa make shallow burrows in peaty soils. The largest known golden mole, the giant golden mole, lives in the forests of the east Cape, South Africa. Here, it most frequently digs burrows around the bases of bushes and shrubs, and will use mole rat burrows if it has the opportunity. Desert golden moles generally make few, if any, burrows. ∎

SAFE HAVENS
Nursery and sleeping chambers may be little more than enlarged tunnel sections (below).

FOOD AND FEEDING

Norman Lightfoot/Bruce Coleman Ltd.

Moles are carnivorous by nature, and are largely dependent for their food on creatures that fall into or pass through their tunnel systems. To support this menu, they scavenge carrion such as dead frogs, birds, and even small mammals. The two other methods by which moles may obtain food are by actively digging out prey from the soil and by foraging on the surface. Some species of golden mole feed in this way. The star-nosed mole is the only true mole that regularly forages on the surface.

The rest of the true moles are earthworm specialists, and rely on these abundant creatures for a major part of their diet. They are not particularly delicate eaters, but tend to tear at their food, and then hastily gulp it down, with a minimum amount of chewing. They do, however, exhibit considerable finesse when cleaning earthworms, whose bodies often contain quantities of soil. A mole will often squeeze a captured worm through its paws as it eats it; this removes most of the grit from the meal, and may have evolved as a way of reducing tooth wear.

THE WORMS THAT TURNED

During the autumn and winter moles will gather together excess earthworms, immobilize them by biting off the head segments, and store them in larders for later consumption. Such larders may be within a fortress, within the tunnel walls, or close to one of the nesting chambers. This practice may seem particularly unpleasant, but in fact its outcome often borders on the miraculous. For if the mole has not consumed the full contents of its larder by the spring, the remaining worm segments disperse as the soil

Color illustrations Wendy Bramall/Wildlife Art Agency

temperature rises, since by then the head segments have regenerated into full-grown worms. The quantities of worms stored in such a way can be surprisingly large—over 4.4 lb (2 kg) of earthworms have been recorded from a single fortress.

Despite their fondness for earthworms, however, moles do vary their diets according to what is seasonally available. During the summer, earthworms migrate more deeply into the soil to flee the hot, dry weather, and moles may have to rely on other food items within the soil—typically wireworms, ground beetles and their larvae, leatherjackets, cutworms, and fever fly larvae in the case of the European mole. Moles also tend to be opportunistic, taking food items as they can get them.

As might be expected from the moles' unusual lifestyle, their feeding patterns are different from many other mammals. Living underground, moles

A star-nosed mole (above) sets to work on a worm. Other mole species generally come to the surface to feed only in winter, when the ground is cold and hard and earthworms are scarce.

DIVING DEEP

The Russian desman (above) is large enough to tackle leeches, small fish, and frogs.

MOVING MEALS

In fertile soils, moles can simply sit back and wait for dinner to fall through into their tunnels (left).

are generally protected from predators, and are largely immune to the changes in temperature that affect surface-dwelling mammals. In addition there is little competition for food, which is available at all hours of the day or night. Indeed, the idea of diurnal or nocturnal activity is fairly redundant to a true mole. There are usually three sessions of activity and three sessions of rest, each lasting for three or four hours, during the course of each 24-hour period. This simple pattern of daily activity represents bouts of almost continuous feeding between periods of digestion.

EARTHWORM

BEETLES

SLUGS

Prey illustrations Dan Wright

Golden moles also seem to rely on soil insects, slugs, snails, and earthworms for their diet. The giant earthworm is also a favorite food item—this spectacular invertebrate can grow to several yards in length. Golden moles are highly sensitive to disturbances on the surface, and emerge rapidly from their burrows or from under the sand to snatch beetles, spiders, and moths. De Winton's golden mole and the Namib golden mole will both burst out from below the desert sand to grab legless lizards and small reptiles. The smaller prey items are dragged under the ground to be consumed. Insects are dispatched swiftly with the cheek teeth, whereas snails are first chipped from their shells with the incisors. Cape golden moles apparently find crop fields and nursery gardens irresistible, with their abundant supplies of worms, slugs, and snails. Naturally, this does not endear them much to farmers, as their burrowing spoils the crops.

Golden moles have been known to reduce body temperature and go into a state of torpor, rather similar to that found in bats, during periods of food shortage. For example, Hottentot's golden mole normally follows a regular routine of resting and activity. However, when faced with a scarcity of food it responds by dropping its body temperature from the normal 92.3°F (33.5° C) to a couple of degrees above its surroundings. This reduces the mole's daily energy expenditure by at least 50 percent.

SWIMMING AFTER PREY

Pyrenean desmans forage underwater for aquatic insects such as stone fly, mayfly, and caddis fly larvae, which they are believed to locate by touch, using their long proboscis to root for the prey items under small rocks and stones. A desman rarely dives for more than fifteen seconds; the buoyancy of the air-filled fur coat is so strong that the animal needs to brace itself against a rock or submerged log on the streambed. Desmans groom carefully between dives as the fur needs to be maintained in top condition to insulate against freezing mountain streams.

The Russian desman survives largely on a diet of insect larvae, but also takes a range of small fish, leeches, frogs, and their eggs. It forages throughout the night, but displays peaks of activity at dusk and dawn. The desman is heavily dependent on scent and touch for finding its food, rather than using sight. The proboscislike snout is ever alert to prey and to threats from predators alike, constantly sniffing the air when the animal is out of the water. When the desman submerges, it sweeps its snout

AMBUSH

Despite its lack of external ears, a golden mole can sense the passing of insects on the desert sands over its head. If it emerges rapidly enough, it may strike lucky with its prey (below).

The European mole may eat its own body weight in earthworms every day.

from side to side along the muddy bottom, probing around the roots and stems of aquatic plants, ready to dislodge dragonfly larvae, tadpoles, small frogs, and snails. After seizing its prey, the desman carries it to the surface to deal with it. A typical hunting haunt of the Russian desman is a shallow, stagnant, vegetation-choked pond along a major river valley; males will actively defend such a chosen feeding area against hungry intruders.

BUSY SHREW-MOLES

The shrew-moles show considerable variety in their feeding habits. The American shrew-mole is an agile creature: It can climb up into low bushes, apparently in search of insects. In addition to foraging on the surface, it occasionally digs shallow burrows, and can even swim well. Active by day and night, it eats invertebrates such as earthworms and insects; it has also been known to eat salamanders. The Asiatic shrew-mole, which lives in forest and alpine habitats, is thought to prey on invertebrates, which it grubs up from among the leaf mold on the forest floor. ■

Jane Burton/Bruce Coleman Ltd.

in SIGHT

POISONED BAIT

The most commonly practiced method of ridding farmland of moles involves the use of earthworms covered with strychnine, a powerful poison. However, the mole's habit of squeezing the grit from earthworms before eating them is thought to have hindered such attempts, as the moles would unintentionally wipe off the powdered strychnine salts.

Today water-soluble strychnine salt solution is used instead. This is usually applied onto earthworms, in particular the common large earthworm, *Lumbricus terrestris*, and the worms are then placed in the mole burrows. Baits are applied to deep runs only, however, since poisoned worms close to the surface pose a serious hazard to other wildlife. By the same token, research is currently being conducted into more humane methods of culling the moles.

LIFE CYCLE

In the Northern Hemisphere, most moles give birth during the spring, when food is most abundant and females can produce plenty of milk. The onset of breeding is, rather surprisingly, triggered by the increasing light levels. Moles are subject to light more often than is commonly supposed, for example when they surface to collect nesting materials and push up spoil heaps.

Female moles can breed in their first year. The ovaries are unique among mammals, being made up of two parts. At the start of the breeding season, the part of the ovary that produces eggs enlarges and follicles begin to develop. Other changes at this time include perforation of the vagina and enlargement of the uterus. The female comes into estrus probably for only 24–36 hours, and then produces eggs.

SUBTERRANEAN SEARCH

During February and March, male moles start to venture outside their home ranges, usually digging long, straight tunnels until they reach the burrows of a female. Sometimes these excursions occur above ground. The daily pattern of activity changes at this time, with males becoming increasingly restless. Instead of returning to the nest to sleep after bouts of

TUNNEL OF LOVE
Once the male has dug through to a female's domain, he may need to chase her for some distance before she consents to mate (above).

OVER THE TOP
Juveniles face great peril as they disperse to find new territories; above ground, they are helplessly exposed to enemies (below).

David Thompson/Oxford Scientific Films

feeding, males just "catnap" in their tunnels and dig until exhausted, in a bid to find as many females as possible. The animals usually mate within the burrows; copulation has only occasionally been seen to occur above ground. In spite of the tremendous efforts of the male to seek out his partner, the pair spend only an hour or so together. Having mated with the female, the mole proceeds to seek out further mates.

Gestation lasts for about four weeks. The number of young varies from two to eight in the European mole and several of the North American species, with a litter size of four being typical. Young moles grow and develop rapidly; they increase their weight almost twenty times within the first three weeks of life—typically from 0.12 oz (3.4 g) at birth to 2 oz (56.7 g) at three weeks old.

Even within the nest chamber, these youngsters are at risk from predators; foxes may dig out nests and destroy the entire litter. Predation of young is not confined to the European mole; the American

Moles are born deep down in a snug chamber, where they are confined for more than a month.

GROWING UP

The life of a European mole

NEWBORN MOLES

are blind, naked, and bright red, but soon fade to a healthy pink, and within 9 or 10 days take on a bluish cast when the fur begins to form.

AT 14 DAYS OLD

the coat sprouts from the skin, and within 17 days is complete (above), *but the eyes do not open until about the 22nd day.*

at a stretch. But during these migrations, the young moles are vulnerable to buzzards, barn and tawny owls, and stoats, and many are killed crossing roads.

By the autumn, some young moles will have survived to establish territories of their own. Having done so, a mole will live out its days there, with only minor boundary alterations resulting from changes in food or soil conditions or the disappearance or arrival of neighbors.

DESMANS AND GOLDEN MOLES

Pyrenean desmans mate in March or April, and as they usually form a solid pair bond there is sometimes intense rivalry for mates between existing territory holders and solitary males. At this time of year, males become far more vigorous in the protection of their territories, swimming up and down the river, particularly at the fringes of their domain. Females, meanwhile, seek out a suitable nest site and start to gather nesting material.

After a four-week gestation period, three or four young are born. They do not venture into the open until they are about seven weeks old, remaining within the parents' territory until they are about ten or eleven weeks old. During the time they are in the nest, the female goes out foraging for food while the male defends the territory.

Russian desmans can give birth twice a year, and generally there are between three and five young in each litter. Desmans advertise the boundaries of their territory by scent marking, the strong, musky odor being produced from a gland at the base of the tail. The young remain with the parents over the summer period before dispersing, usually overland, during early autumn. The female builds a nest of her own away from the young soon after they are born, and visits her offspring only to suckle them. The male, on the other hand, takes a more active interest in the young, often sharing the nesting chamber and helping to keep them warm.

The breeding cycle of golden moles is little studied. It is known that one of the most studied species, the Cape golden mole, mates during the rainy season from April to July, and that the two offspring are suckled in a circular nest made of leaves. ■

coast mole frequently loses young to a snake known as the rubber boa. Probably more importantly, any food shortage at this critical time may cause whole litters to starve to death.

Having spent about a month in the nest, the young moles are ready to venture out for the first time, but they generally stay within the home territory until ten weeks old. Local populations of moles may triple during May and June, when the young at first emerge from the nest, and dispersion quickly follows. They usually move above ground to seek new territories, and will even swim open stretches of water, paddling gamely for as long as fifty minutes

FROM BIRTH TO DEATH

EUROPEAN MOLE	PYRENEAN DESMAN
GESTATION: 35–42 DAYS	**GESTATION:** 3–4 WEEKS
LITTER SIZE: 2–9	**LITTER SIZE:** 1–5
WEIGHT AT BIRTH: 0.1 OZ (3.8 G)	**WEIGHT AT BIRTH:** UNKNOWN
WEANING: 2 MONTHS	**WEANING:** UNKNOWN
SEXUAL MATURITY: 10–12 MONTHS	**SEXUAL MATURITY:** 12 MONTHS
LONGEVITY IN WILD: 3–4 YEARS	**LONGEVITY IN WILD:** 4 YEARS

Color illustrations Wayne Ford/Wildlife Art Agency

POISONED FOR THEIR PELTS

LIFE HAS NOT BEEN EASY FOR THE HUMBLE MOLE: ITS SOFT BUT TOUGH LITTLE PELT WAS ONCE A FAVORITE OF THE FUR TRADERS, AND ITS UGLY SPOIL HEAPS CONTINUE TO INFURIATE LANDOWNERS EVERYWHERE

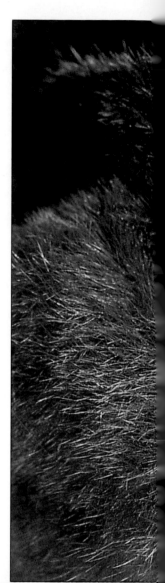

Moles have been hunted and traded for hundreds of years. The use of moleskin in hats and other apparel originated as early as Roman times, albeit to a limited extent. With the passing ages, moleskin entered more widespread trade.

Landowners were eager to rid themselves of the unsightly spoil heaps of a mole infestation, and many English parishes hired professional molecatchers to rid the fields of moles. Some of these molecatchers claimed to take a thousand or more moles each winter. The tiny pelts were stitched into coats, waistcoats, children's caps, purses, and tobacco pouches for the rural gentry from the 17th century well into the 19th century.

MOLESKINS WERE VALUED FOR TRADE ACCORDING TO THEIR SIZE AND WHETHER THEY SHOWED SIGNS OF MOLT

The fur was in particularly heavy demand during the last decade of the 19th century; later on, in 1904, about one million skins were offered for sale on the London market alone. Around 20 percent of these came from Germany, where the slump in mole numbers resulted in concern being expressed for the very survival of the species. A parallel industry evolved in North America, based in particular upon Townsend's mole. The industry declined during the First World War, but recovered strongly to incorporate an American market during the 1920s. Once again, Germany was a major exporter of moleskins.

Since these boom times, wearing moleskins has become steadily less fashionable and synthetic furs have more or less cornered the market. But it is still instructive to examine how mole-trapping on such a grand scale affected population levels. Biologists have studied this using computer modeling.

They compared a realistic model of a population subject only to natural mortality with models of populations in which molecatchers operated at varying rates, taking 5 and 10 percent of the population in addition to the moles that would die of natural causes. The results indicated that even low levels of trapping could cause marked decreases in the density of a mole population. The intense levels of exploitation that occurred in Europe during the late 19th and early 20th centuries must have had a severe effect on mole populations. Fortunately, these engaging creatures are more than capable of surviving such decimation; indeed, they are one of our most abundant small mammals.

Despite its reputation as a pest, the European mole (right) *causes little actual damage to crops.*

Laurie Campbell/NHPA

A mole gibbet (above). *Moles are particularly unpopular with farmers and gardners.*

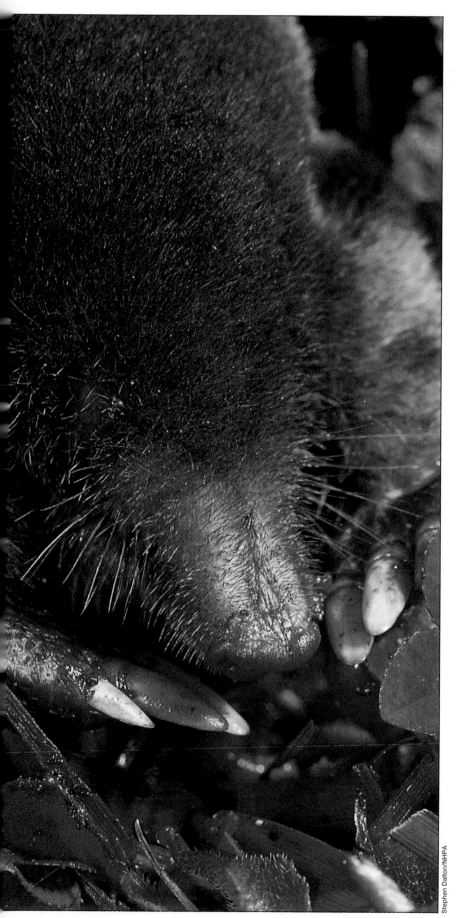

Stephen Dalton/NHPA

*This map shows the current range of
the giant golden mole.*

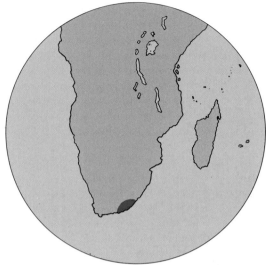

GIANT GOLDEN MOLE

The rare giant golden mole has a severely limited distribution within South Africa. It lives in dry forests within the Transkei and Ciskei republics, and the forest blocks in which it lives are slowly succumbing to the pressure of domestic grazing stock or to economic development.

Today, moles can still be legally trapped and poisoned in England, although authority to purchase and use strychnine in mole removal has to be issued by the Ministry of Agriculture, Fisheries, and Food (MAFF). Many farmers and gardeners regard moles as pests. In fact, the damage that is actually attributable to mole activity is slight, although the extent of damage to newly cultivated areas may have adverse financial implications at a local level—on hill farms and smallholdings, for example. In the British Isles, the most important type of damage is the contamination by molehills of the grass used to make silage. Too much soil in silage causes poor fermentation and poor preservation of the silage.

DESMAN PELTS

The Russian desman, too, was heavily hunted for its coat. Indeed, a large part of our early knowledge of the desman's lifestyle came from observations and records from trappers. The soft, dense fur of this species has always been highly prized among local people, but a flourishing export trade in the latter part of the 19th century had a more serious impact upon desman numbers.

John Hartley/Jersey Wildlife Preservation Trust

(in)SIGHT

PYRENEAN PROBLEMS

Although the Pyrenean desman is not at risk from trappers, being generally found at low densities and proving difficult to trap, it is vulnerable to the misguided persecution it receives from anglers, who believe that it competes with them for fish, and, until recently, from the overzealous activities of museum collectors.

Historically, dam projects, road building, and human persecution caused the decline of this species. More recently, the salting of winter roads to melt snow is polluting the mountain streams in which the desman lives. Pollution not only depletes the desman's prey, but also reduces its ability to keep its fur in a waterproof condition. If its underfur remains wet, a desman may rapidly die of hypothermia.

Another recent threat is the introduction of the American mink to some areas of northern Spain. This alien species, which is thought to have escaped from mink farms in around 1982, may be killing and displacing desmans in some areas, in addition to having a devastating effect on fish and small bird populations.

The plight of the Russian desman even attracted the attention of naturalist Gerald Durrell.

Russian desmans were comparatively easy to catch. One hunter would scare the creature from its bankside home, and it would then be clubbed to death by a second hunter. At certain times of the year, Russian desmans are temporarily flooded out of their burrows, notably during the spring thaw, making them easier to catch. Consequently, April and May became prime times to hunt desmans. Other methods of capture included shooting the unfortunate creatures as they emerged to feed, or setting snares at the underwater entrances to their burrows. There are records of hunters bringing 400–500 pelts to market on just one day, and by the turn of the century about 20,000 skins were being processed annually.

After the First World War, desman hunting declined sharply, and numbers recovered to some degree. The Russian desman is now protected by law, and today over 50,000 of these resilient creatures live in the river basins of the Volga, its tributaries, and many other rivers. ■

MOLES AND DESMANS IN DANGER

MOST GOLDEN MOLE SPECIES ARE CLASSIFIED AS *INSUFFICIENTLY KNOWN*, MEANING THERE IS NOT ENOUGH INFORMATION FOR THE INTERNATIONAL UNION FOR THE CONSERVATION OF NATURE (IUCN), OR THE WORLD CONSERVATION UNION, TO CLASSIFY THE ANIMAL WITH ANY DEGREE OF ACCURACY.

GOLDEN MOLES CLASSIFIED AS INSUFFICIENTLY KNOWN:
GUNNING • ZULU • SCHLATER • JULIANA • VISAGIE • VAN ZYL • DE WINTON • ROUGH-HAIRED • SOMALI

GOLDEN MOLES CLASSIFIED AS RARE:
DUTHRIE • YELLOW • GIANT • GRANT

RUSSIAN DESMAN	VULNERABLE
PYRENEAN DESMAN	VULNERABLE
SADO MOLE	RARE

VULNERABLE MEANS THAT THE SPECIES MAY BECOME ENDANGERED IF ACTION IS NOT TAKEN TO PRESERVE IT. THE TERM *RARE* IS APPLIED TO SPECIES THAT ARE NOT ENDANGERED OR VULNERABLE, BUT THAT ARE AT RISK.

INTO THE FUTURE

Although some species, notably the European mole, are still common and widespread, others are facing a struggle for survival in a world increasingly dominated by humankind. A major problem is that so little is known about these animals. The precise ranges of, for example, the Kansu mole of China and the greater Japanese mole and its relatives are not documented.

The prospects for the two species of desman look bleak. Their precise distribution is unknown, but it is certain that, for the Pyrenean desman in particular, an already limited range is steadily shrinking and breaking up. Every year more dams are built, more mountain roads are carved across what were once remote, wild areas, causing disturbance and pollution when the roads are salted in winter, and more and more animals are trapped for private collectors. Because the Pyrenean desman depends so

PREDICTION

MIXED PROSPECTS

The fate of certain species of golden mole, and of the desmans, looks highly perilous. The European mole, however, is assured of a safe future now that trade in its pelt has all but ceased.

absolutely on a single, highly specific habitat, the multiple threats can easily wipe out entire populations along the more vulnerable mountain streams.

Fortunately, scientists are beginning to learn a little more about the elusive Pyrenean desman. Researchers are following animals in the field as they move about at night, tagging individuals with tiny radio transmitters or lightweight backpacks filled with phosphorescent gelatine capsules.

Good numbers in the Volga River basins and other progress are positive signs for the Russian desman. Conservationists are learning more about its biology and about the conditions it needs to thrive in special sites such as the Oka Reserve, some 310 miles (500 km) southeast of Moscow. Here, 700–1,400 desmans live in the preserve's patchwork of small lakes and oxbow ponds. Part of the preserve is landscaped to provide ideal desman habitat. In addition, the Russian desman has been reintroduced into some areas of the former Soviet Union from which it had disappeared, such as the Dneipr and upper Ob river systems. ∎

SPECIMEN HUNTERS

Surprisingly, one threat to the already beleaguered populations of the Pyrenean desman has come from the natural history sections of certain museums and from university zoology departments in Spain. Nowadays, the practice of collecting as many specimens as possible of an animal, with a view to providing research material for future studies on its classification and general biology, is largely regarded as wasteful—especially with such threatened species as the Pyrenean desman.

Despite this—and in defiance of their full legal protection by the Spanish government—there have been several reports of large numbers of desmans being killed and stockpiled by disreputable museums and laboratories. Collection methods include "electrofishing," in which the animals are easily stunned or killed—along with every other creature in the surrounding waters. During the late 1980s, more than seventy dried skins were found in the laboratory of a university professor who did not even carry out research on desmans.

ACTION FOR DESMANS

One good reason for saving the Pyrenean desman is that its presence is an indicator of water quality in what is left of Europe's threatened mountain streams. If the desman is to be saved, it is vital to continue and step up research. The main priorities are to produce accurate censuses of the scattered populations that remain, establish the degree to which mink compete for food and possibly prey on the desman itself, and minimize other threats that range from persecution by anglers to the effects of afforestation.

Illustration Evi Antoniou

CEBID MONKEYS

Cebid monkeys belong to the Primate order. Other primates include:

LEMURS

GALAGOS

TARSIERS

MARMOSETS

TAMARINS

OLD WORLD MONKEYS

APES & HUMAN

Gregory G. Dimijian/Oxford Scientific Films

THERE HANGS A TAIL

FORESTS ACROSS TROPICAL AMERICA ARE THE DOMAIN OF THE CEBID MONKEYS, WHOSE DAZZLING DIVERSITY IS SHOWN NOT JUST IN THEIR DIET BUT ALSO IN HOW THEY MOVE ABOUT THE TREETOPS

The cebid monkeys are among the most numerous of mammals that reside in the luxuriant tropical forests of the Americas. So successful have they been in their ecologically rich environment that they have evolved into many different forms, with distinctiveness echoed in their common names: capuchins, squirrel and night monkeys, titi monkeys, uakaris, sakis and bearded sakis, howler monkeys, woolly monkeys, spider monkeys, and woolly spider monkeys. Like all monkeys, they are active, agile creatures capable of moving with speed and poise through the tree crowns as they search for food and steer clear of danger.

These monkeys live only in the Americas, while their counterparts—the macaques, guenons, langurs, and baboons—are limited to Africa and Asia. These two separate groups are often called the New World and the Old World monkeys. The geographical distinction is reinforced by key anatomical differences:

Carol Farneti/Planet Earth Pictures

TELLING TAILS

Four of the larger types of cebid monkeys possess something no other primates have: a prehensile tail. Such a tail is capable of gripping objects as if it were an extra hand. Spider monkeys, woolly monkeys, woolly spider monkeys, and howler monkeys all use their long, muscular tails to help them move about the trees and to grip objects otherwise out of reach. The monkeys can even swing or hang with only the tail wrapped around a branch, leaving arms and legs free.

In all four genera, the underside of the tail is bare near the tip, revealing a patch of soft, ridged skin. This not only provides grip but is also sensitive to touch, enabling the animal to use its tail to investigate objects such as fruit before grasping them. Capuchin monkeys also have a gripping tail, but to a lesser degree: They use it mainly as a prop while traveling.

Alan Root/Survival Anglia

The nostrils, for example, are more widely spaced in the New World monkeys, which are consequently referred to by many zoologists as the platyrrhine (PLAT-ee-rine), or flat-nosed monkeys.

Tens of millions of years ago, platyrrhine monkeys arrived in what was then the island continent of South America. They probably crossed the oceans on floating vegetation, and those that survived their unexpected voyage were introduced to a forested land devoid of any other primates. In the absence of competition the newcomers flourished, dispersed, and rapidly diversified.

There are two major groups among today's platyrrhine monkeys. One is the cebid monkeys, the other consists of the marmosets and tamarins—small-bodied, frisky animals with claws rather than nails. Both have become widespread in tropical South America, and when a land bridge formed with the northern continent five or six million years ago they spread into Central America.

Despite all their many variations in physiology and lifestyle, there are important traits that all of the

---

NIGHT MONKEYS HAVE HUGE, OWL-LIKE EYES, WHICH FUNCTION FULLY EVEN IN THE GLIMMER OF MOONLIGHT AND STARS

---

cebid monkeys share. As well as the distinctive nose shape, they lack cheek pouches, they possess six cheek teeth per jaw, and have flat nails, rather than claws, on the digits. They lack the rump callouses and opposable thumbs of some other monkeys, but they share the same basic body plan of slender, flexible torso, rounded head, and long limbs. Their physique enables them to walk and climb on branches, suspend themselves from them, and leap between trees. Cebid monkeys, however, are not well adapted for walking on flat surfaces and seldom spend long periods on the ground.

Like Old World monkeys, platyrrhines have large brains, manual dexterity, and forward-facing eyes that can judge distances. These traits combine both to foster an inquisitiveness toward the environment and to give the animals the hand-eye coordination that enables them to investigate and handle objects. The eyes are also relatively large, with well-developed eyelids, and rods and cones are arranged on the retina of the eye as in humans, permitting color vision as well as the detection of light and shade. Only the night monkeys or douroucoulis lack retinal cones and so do not have color vision, but since they are active after dark they do not need it. ∎

The female white-faced saki lacks the distinctive facial markings of her mate.

THE CEBID MONKEYS' FAMILY TREE

Because of the broadened shape of their noses, New World monkeys are sometimes collectively referred to as the platyrrhines. Though a mixed group, with six subfamilies, the cebid monkeys are distinctly different from their neighboring platyrrhines, the marmosets and tamarins.

TITI MONKEYS

Callicebus
(*cah-lee-SEE-buss*)

The long, dense fur of these little monkeys makes them seem thicker in body than they are—particularly because their heads are so small and rounded. There are up to thirteen titi species ranging across Amazonia and southeast Brazil.

WOOLLY MONKEYS

Lagothrix
(*LAH-go-thricks*)

These large, thickset monkeys have a long tail and short, dense fur. As in spider and howler monkeys, the tail is prehensile. There are two species distributed patchily across western Amazonia.

NIGHT MONKEY

SQUIRREL MONKEY

RED OUAKARI

1410

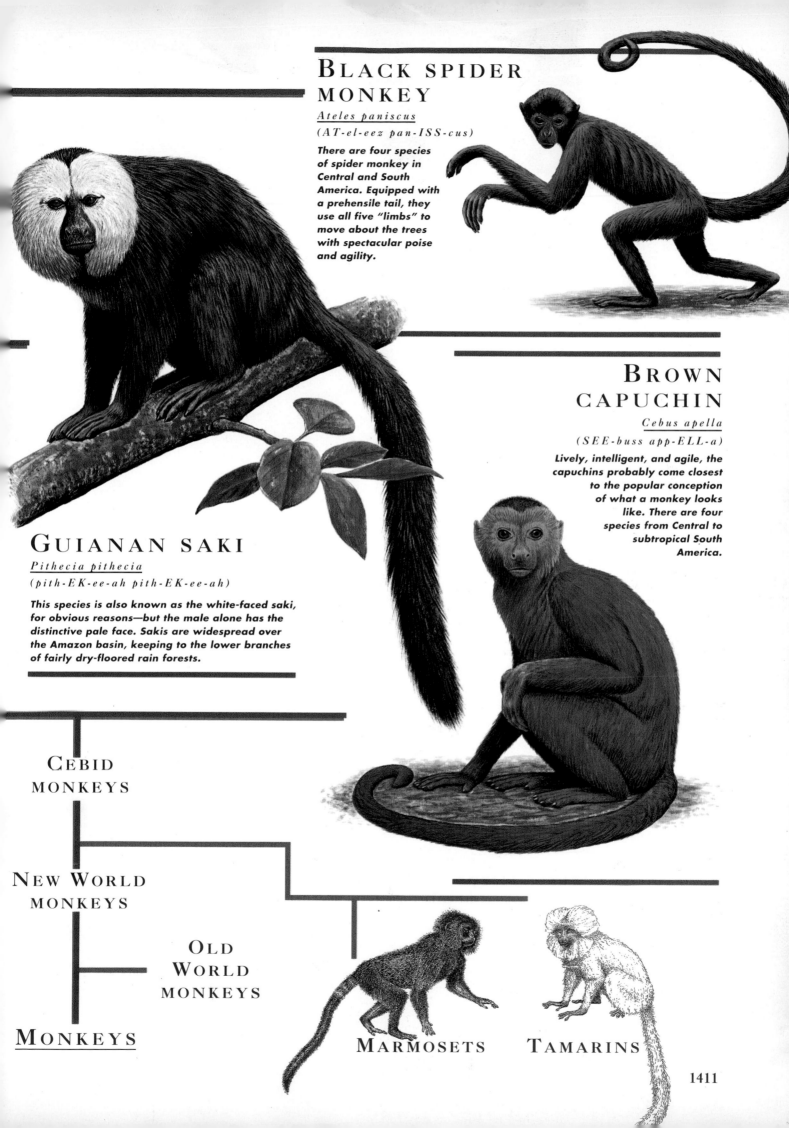

BLACK SPIDER MONKEY

Ateles paniscus
(AT-el-eez pan-ISS-cus)

There are four species of spider monkey in Central and South America. Equipped with a prehensile tail, they use all five "limbs" to move about the trees with spectacular poise and agility.

BROWN CAPUCHIN

Cebus apella
(SEE-buss app-ELL-a)

Lively, intelligent, and agile, the capuchins probably come closest to the popular conception of what a monkey looks like. There are four species from Central to subtropical South America.

GUIANAN SAKI

Pithecia pithecia
(pith-EK-ee-ah pith-EK-ee-ah)

This species is also known as the white-faced saki, for obvious reasons—but the male alone has the distinctive pale face. Sakis are widespread over the Amazon basin, keeping to the lower branches of fairly dry-floored rain forests.

CEBID
MONKEYS

NEW WORLD
MONKEYS

OLD
WORLD
MONKEYS

MONKEYS

MARMOSETS   TAMARINS

1411

ANATOMY: THE CAPUCHIN

The woolly spider monkey (above left) measures 18–25 in (46–63 cm) from head to rump, with a tail 25.5–29 in (65–74 cm) long. The squirrel monkey (above right) has a head-and-body length of 10–14.5 in (25–37 cm), and a tail length of 14.5–17.5 in (37–44.5 cm).

SQUIRREL MONKEY

MONK SAKI

RED HOWLER MONKEY

Some of the diversity within the cebid monkeys can be seen simply in a look at facial features. The neat little squirrel monkey has a facial "mask" on its short, broad muzzle; the monk saki's face is framed by full, shaggy hair and two white jaw streaks, while the red howler has a naked face.

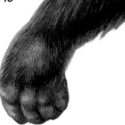

THE ARMS

are lithe and short but well muscled. A young capuchin can grasp its mother's fur immediately after birth, and soon learns to use its limbs to swing about the branches.

HIND FOOT

Like many primates, capuchins have an opposable big toe, which improves their grip on branches. Despite this, capuchins are rarely seen seated in a tree without their tail tip locked around a branch to give a third point of contact and support.

SKELETON

The skeleton of a white-faced capuchin shows the slender form, long legs, and long balance-aiding tail typical of agile, tree-climbing monkeys, for whom maneuverability is key and great weight would be a distinct liability.

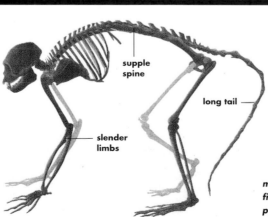

supple spine

slender limbs

long tail

CAPUCHIN HAND

long thumb

long, fine bones

Capuchins have nimble hands, and as such were widely used in the past in scientific research. Many apes, and New World monkeys too, have thumbs that are short in proportion to the fingers: This enables a strong "hook grip" on branches but provides little finesse when handling objects or using tools. The capuchin, however, has a comparatively functional thumb.

X-ray illustrations Elisabeth Smith

FACE FUR

Capuchin monkeys have distinctive fur on the head and face. The brown capuchin is notable for developing prominent tufts or horns of fur over the eyes or on top of the head. The white-faced capuchin, by contrast, develops a ruff of long white hairs around the face. The name capuchin derives from the likeness of the monkey's black cap to the hood, or "capuche," of Franciscan monks.

THE BODY

is fairly small but robust. Cebid monkeys differ greatly not just in shape and coloration but also in body size. The largest of them—indeed, the largest primate in the Americas—is the woolly spider monkey or muriqui. The smallest are the dainty squirrel monkeys. A full-size woolly spider monkey may weigh twelve times as much as a typical squirrel monkey.

THE TAIL

Is long and, to a moderate degree, prehensile; it lacks the naked undertip present on fully prehensile-tailed species. Capuchins often carry their tails curled tightly at the tip, which has earned them the alternative name of ring-tail monkeys.

FACT FILE:

WHITE-FACED CAPUCHIN

CLASSIFICATION

GENUS: CEBUS
SPECIES: CAPUCINUS

SIZE

HEAD–BODY LENGTH: 12.5–18 IN (32–46 CM)
TAIL LENGTH: 16–20 IN (40–50 CM)
WEIGHT: 4.5–8.5 LB (2–3.8 KG)

COLORATION

FUR ON UNDERSIDES, UPPER LIMBS, AND FACE CREAM TO WHITE; ELSEWHERE, INCLUDING CAP, GRADING TO BLACK

FEATURES

ROUNDED HEAD
FORWARD-FACING EYES
SLENDER, AGILE BUILD
MEDIUM-SHORT LIMBS AND LONG, FLEXIBLE, SEMIPREHENSILE TAIL
MALE SLIGHTLY LARGER THAN FEMALE
DISTINCTIVE BLACK CAP
WHITE FACIAL RUFF ON OLDER INDIVIDUALS

CAPUCHIN SKULL AND JAW

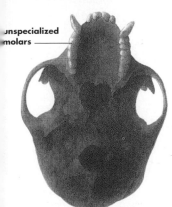

unspecialized molars

The teeth and jaws give strong clues to the diet of different monkeys. Large jaws and broad, flat teeth give the crushing power needed for chewing coarse plants. Those monkeys that eat insects have sharp, narrow teeth for piercing exoskeletons and cutting the prey up quickly.

stout canines

CAPUCHIN SKULL

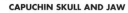

large braincase

TITI SKULL

forward-facing eye sockets

The skulls of cebid monkeys show the large braincase and forward-facing eye sockets typical of primates. These relatively intelligent animals rely on forward vision so that they can make accurate leaps from branch to branch.

WOOLLY MONKEY SKULL

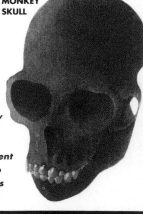

TROOPS IN THE TREES

AGAINST THE BACKDROP OF THE TROPICAL FOREST, WITH ITS MANY LEVELS FROM THE UNDERSTORY TO THE HIGH CANOPY, CEBID MONKEYS PLAY OUT THE COMPLEX DRAMA OF THEIR LIVES

Although it is hard to generalize across this group of animals, there are some common patterns in the behavior of cebid monkeys. All are arboreal, and most live in dense forest. All but one genus are active in daylight hours, and most live in territorial family units, exhibit complicated social behavior, and communicate with sounds and gestures.

Each day's activities generally begin at daybreak, when the monkey troop emerges from its sleeping site. A bout of social activity typically starts the day off, followed by periods of feeding, resting, and further social engagement, until dusk starts to fall, and the animals return to their sleeping sites. Studies of mantled howler monkeys in Panama showed that a troop will wake at dawn high in a tree and begin their day with a chorus of territorial roaring. A period of rest follows, and then the animals feed close to their sleeping area before moving out to their main foraging sites. Before noon, most feeding has ceased. Thereafter the animals rest until midafternoon, feed a little more, and then return to the sleeping tree, calling to their distant neighbors as they go.

Howler monkeys commonly spend up to three-quarters of the day resting. Other species, though not quite so leisurely, also have long rest periods. Squirrel monkeys typically rest for one or two hours at midday. Titi monkeys feed intensively only in the early morning and from midafternoon, and while resting they perch close together, often with tails entwined. Night monkeys also tend to have a long break in their activities, but being nocturnal, theirs is likely to be around midnight. They spend the day huddled among dense foliage, woody vines, or in tree holes, emerging at twilight to begin their foraging and returning to their sleeping sites at dawn.

Safe shelter during daylight is essential for the night monkey, for like many of the smaller species it can be vulnerable to predators. Since they are agile and alert, monkeys are not easy for climbing animals to catch, but they are at risk from birds of prey. The harpy and crested eagles are particularly skilled at snatching squirrel monkeys, titi monkeys, sakis, and capuchins from the treetops. The sight of almost any large bird winging over the trees is enough to send troops of brown capuchins scurrying in alarm.

Safety is probably a major reason why few monkeys spend much time on the forest floor. Squirrel monkeys, brown capuchins, and black howler monkeys descend to forage sometimes, but they are too awkward and vulnerable to dally there for long. A walking spider monkey is forced to teeter erect on its legs with its long spindly arms held upright. But this animal's awkwardness on the ground is overshadowed by its sheer acrobatic grace in the branches where it belongs.

The male white-faced saki is most unlike his mate, who lacks the distinctive mask (above).

Red ouakaris may seem to us to be outrageously ugly, but they are gentle, peaceable animals.

Spider monkeys epitomize one form of monkey agility. With five long limbs at their disposal—including the tail—they can hang at any angle from branches, often anchored solely by the tail. Rapid movement through the canopy is by a gibbonlike swinging, with hands alternately taking hold and arms stretching wide to pull the animal across gaps.

Squirrel monkeys run along branches on all fours with great nimbleness and speed, bounding deftly through dense vegetation. White-faced sakis are not as restless as the squirrel monkeys, but when the need arises they can vacate a tree fast, galloping along branches and launching themselves between supports up to 33 ft (10 m) apart. Little wonder this species is also known as the "flying monkey." ■

The titi's long tail (above) *is not truly prehensile, but is used in displays of affection with others.*

HABITATS

Between them, the cebid monkeys range over most of tropical America and into subtropical South America. Though cebids are occasionally spotted on the ground, foraging, playing, drinking from streams, or crossing open spaces, they are creatures expressly designed for life in the trees. And although most of them live in the tree crowns, where outspreading branches meet to form the rain forest canopy, they are surely the most conspicuous of mammals in their luxuriant habitat—not always visible, but frequently noisy. The canopy is where they find their sustenance and secure shelter, where they interact and breed. For the most part, their habitat is tropical evergreen forest grading to sub-tropical rain forests in the south, and montane and cloud forests on higher ground. In these moist, rich habitats the densities of some species reach high levels. Densities of over 259 animals per square mile (100 per square kilometer) have been recorded for howler monkeys, while the diminutive squirrel monkeys have been recorded at densities of over 1,300 per square mile (500 per square kilometer) in the Peruvian Amazon.

ATLANTIC FOREST

Brazil's Atlantic Forest was once a mixture of dense lowland rain forest and more broken mountain forests. The forest that remains today, after much deforestation, is mostly montane, and especially rich in palms, bromeliads, and tree ferns. Many of the trees are anchored by great buttressed trunks. As well as providing a home for widespread South American animals such as jaguars, anteaters, tapirs, macaws, and boas, the forest patches are last refuges for hundreds of frogs, birds, and mammals. Several species, such as the woolly spider monkey, the brown howler monkey, and the masked titi, are found only in these forest fragments.

Nick Gordon/Ardea

DISTRIBUTION

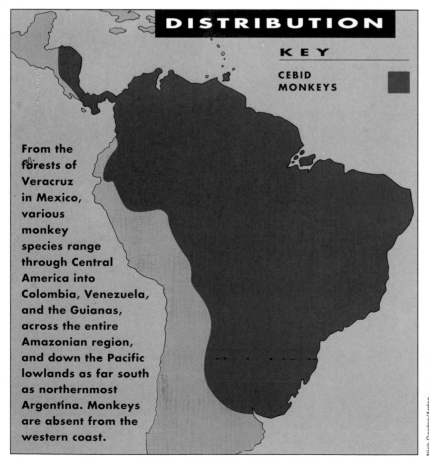

KEY

CEBID MONKEYS

From the forests of Veracruz in Mexico, various monkey species range through Central America into Colombia, Venezuela, and the Guianas, across the entire Amazonian region, and down the Pacific lowlands as far south as northernmost Argentina. Monkeys are absent from the western coast.

Nick Gordon/Ardea

continuous forest and broken savanna woodland, but they have also been recorded at elevations of 10,500 ft (3,200 m) in the Andes, they survive in areas in the south of their range where temperatures occasionally fall below freezing, and they often dwell quite close to human settlements. In the dry thorn woods of the Paraguayan Chaco, where their principal enemies, daytime-flying eagles, are rare, but another, the great horned owl, is common, night monkeys have actually modified their behavior so that they do some of their foraging in daylight.

But at the other end of the scale are many species confined to lowland rain-forest habitats and others with extremely specialized and localized habitats. Both species of ouakari live in wedge-shaped portions of the western Amazon, where riverside forests experience deep seasonal flooding. The monkeys seem all but confined to these swamp forest habitats. In such an environ-

NEW WORLD MONKEYS ARE FOUND IN SUCH DIVERSE HABITATS AS THORN SCRUB, SAVANNA, AND CLOUD FOREST

ment, arboreal locomotion is an essential ability for mammals. The yellow-tailed woolly monkey is one of the most limited in range of any monkey species. It occurs only in a small region of cloud forest on the flanks of the Andes in northern Peru.

Differences are also apparent in the ways different species utilize the forest habitat. Though there are species like the brown capuchin, which roam quite widely from the lowest vegetation up to the top of the canopy, others spend the bulk of their time at distinct levels. Bearded sakis, ouakaris, and spider monkeys, for example, prefer to keep high up in the canopy, while squirrel monkeys are much more at home in the understory, in shrubs, or in dense "jungle" vegetation at the forest edge.

In many areas, different preferences such as these enable several different types of monkeys to coexist in the same habitat even though they might have similar diets. Competition between species in the same genus, though, tends to be so great because of similarity in ecological niches that they seldom coexist. Dusky titis and yellow-handed titis overlap in range extensively in the western Amazon, but while the former prefers swampy, riverside forests the latter keeps to forest on higher ground that is never flooded. Where similar species do coexist, as in the case of the brown capuchin, which overlaps with other capuchins, there is usually a clear distinction between the species in diet. The brown capuchin tends to have a much more vegetarian diet than its counterparts. ∎

As well as the Amazon Basin, there is another huge region of Brazil in which the natural vegetation is tropical rain forest. From the states of Rio Grande do Norte in the northeast to Rio Grande do Sul in the south, a vast belt of land paralleling the Atlantic Ocean used to be clothed in greenery. Known as the Atlantic Forest, it was an ecosystem entirely separate from the Amazonian forests, with an unimaginable variety of endemic plants and animals (species that do not occur elsewhere). Today, precious little of the Atlantic Forest remains, but the pockets that do exist still exhibit the wildlife richness and exuberant grandeur of the habitat.

SAVANNA MONKEYS

Dense forests are by no means the only habitat utilized by cebid monkeys. Some of the more adaptable species, such as the red howler monkey and the weeper capuchin, venture into savanna woodlands where there are pronounced dry seasons. Squirrel monkeys and capuchins also occur in coastal mangrove swamps, the lower levels of which are invaded by seawater whenever the tide is high.

Perhaps the most tolerant of all in habitat terms are the night monkeys. Not only do they occur in

Woolly monkeys are fruit-eating inhabitants of tropical and montane Amazonian forests.

FOOD AND FEEDING

Between them, cebid monkeys make use of the full range of food sources the rain forest has to offer. Most of the species eat both plant and animal food to some extent, although one or a few types of food tend to form the bulk of their diet. The woolly spider monkey, for example, is predominantly a leaf-eater, supplementing its diet mainly with fruits and flowers. Howler monkeys also gain about half of their intake from leaves. Fruit, a less abundant but more nutritious food source, is the principal food of sakis, woolly monkeys, and spider monkeys, and the bearded saki has specially shaped, strong dentition that enables it to break open hard nuts in its jaws. Squirrel monkeys, on the other hand, rely quite heavily on insects and spiders, and can survive on a wholly insectivorous diet.

Night monkeys and capuchins enjoy very mixed diets. A night or day's foraging might yield fruits, nuts, berries, seeds, flowers, shoots, leaves, bark, roots, gums, insects, spiders, snails, birds' eggs, frogs, and lizards. Capuchins may also forage on the seashore, collecting oysters or crabs; they sometimes catch squirrels in the trees, and have been reported to prey on other, smaller monkeys such as titis and

Black-capped capuchins are dexterous feeders, and will even extract frogs out of holes in a trunk.

AMAZING FACTS

● **Capuchins are recognized to be among the most intelligent of monkeys, as shown in some of their feeding behavior. When eating, the monkeys often place their lower arms close together, making a "table" with which to catch and retrieve any morsels that fall from their mouths. When squeezing large fruit, they hold their heads back to avoid the squirt of juices.**

● **Capuchins smash nuts against hard objects or each other in order to get to the kernel, and captive monkeys have been observed selecting and using tools to hammer nuts open.**

SHARED RESOURCES

The dusky titi monkey (abov avoids competing for food w relative the white-handed ti eating a subtly different die fruit and leaves, rather than fruit and insects.

squirrel monkeys. Sakis also have a taste for verte-brates, including small birds, mice, and roosting bats, which they tear apart in their hands before eating.

Some types of food are more demanding on the digestive system than others. Vegetation usually takes longer to digest than insect food, requiring more stomach space to store the food while it is processed. Leaves are particularly difficult since

François Gohier/Ardea

HAND-PICKING HOWLERS
Red howler monkeys do most of their foraging in the middle and lower parts of the canopy where they eat leaves as well as fruit.

MIDNIGHT SNACK
The douroucouli or night monkey avoids competition with other monkeys by feeding during the hours of darkness (above left).

ACROBAT
The black spider monkey makes full use of its tail when feeding, especially when among thin branches (left).

Brian Edwards/Wildlife Art Agency

they contain so much fibrous cellulose—a substance that cannot be digested without special help. Howler monkeys cope with a leafy diet because they have enlarged sections of the gut containing bacteria that can steadily break down and release the energy in cellulose.

A large stomach requires a large body to carry it around, and there is indeed a rough correlation among the cebid monkeys between size and diet. Larger species, by and large, are the more vegetarian. Smaller body size not only means that stomach size and digestion periods are limited, it also limits the size and strength of jaws for coping with large or tough-skinned fruit. Small monkeys therefore tend to forage for food that is easily eaten and easily digested, such as insects, berries, and ripe fruit. But since these animals are small and their energy requirements therefore lower they can afford to forage for such food that requires more searching but is easily processed. Although patterns of foraging vary widely within each species, it is noteworthy that squirrel monkeys do tend to cover more distance—up to 2.5 miles (4 km) in each day's foraging—than bigger, more vegetarian monkeys such as howlers, for which movements of 0.6 miles (1 km) per day would be exceptional.

Many cebid monkeys feed in company. Sociable monkeys tend to leave their sleeping sites in foraging parties. These are closeknit in squirrel monkeys, which tend to move as a unit, searching avidly for insects and other items but passing on before they have exhausted the supply in any one tree. Capuchin groups, on the other hand, tend to be more dispersed as they forage, both vertically and horizontally, through the trees. It is not uncommon for members of the same group to wander 660 ft (200 m) apart as they search for food. ∎

SOCIAL STRUCTURE

D. & R. Sullivan/Bruce Coleman Ltd.

Monkeys are inherently sociable animals, nearly always encountered in groups, and cebid monkeys are certainly no exception. But the size and social structure of troops sharing the tropical forests of the Americas varies in crucial ways. The key distinction is between species that tend to be polygamous and travel in groups containing a number of mature adults and those that are monogamous and live in smaller groups led by an adult pair.

Most species fall firmly into the first category, and are typically sighted in groups of from five to thirty individuals, although some, such as the common woolly monkey, form groups up to seventy strong. In situations where the overall population is thinly spread, capuchins and howler monkeys may live in small bands consisting of one adult male, a few adult females and their young, but in other circumstances groups of ten to twenty are the norm, with several males associating together.

For woolly monkeys and ouakaris, groups typically contain a mixture of adult and subadult females, adult and subadult males, and a retinue of offspring of various ages. Females in the group mate most readily with males that have a high status, but they will also approach subordinate males. Each group occupies a joint home range, which in the common woolly monkey may be over four square miles (ten square kilometers) in area.

Spider monkeys socialize in a slightly different way. Large groups of them—up to eighty strong in the black-handed spider monkey—occupy distinct

Red howlers (above) *live in groups led by males, who are ranked by age. They howl in the morning to proclaim the extent of their territory.*

TINY, BUT MANY
Squirrel monkey groups (right) *vary in size according to the habitat: They reach their maximum in areas of virgin rain forest. Social ties within such groups are often highly complex.*

Stephen Message/Wildlife Art Agency

in SIGHT

SOCIAL PAIRS?

Recent studies suggest that the bearded saki might have a social pattern quite unlike that of any other monkey. Groups of these monkeys that have been observed in the wild contain roughly equal numbers of adult males and females—for example, one group of twenty-five consisted of eight adult males, nine adult females, and eight juveniles.

While foraging, this group often split up into subgroups of one adult male, an adult female, and a couple of young. There is therefore the possibility that the group is a community of monogamous pairs and their young. If so, the bearded saki would be the only primate known to live in such a society—apart from human beings.

sections of forest, but for most of the time they split up into subgroups of fluid composition. Members of subgroups often change when two bands meet up, and now and again the entire group coalesces in one place. Squirrel monkey groups, which are similar sized, assemble together every night for sleeping. By day they, too, tend to split into foraging subgroups, but with divisions that are more clearcut. Males are usually forced to forage separately from females, and all-female bands tend to separate from females with young.

CONFRONTATION

When spider monkey subgroups from the same group encounter one another, recognition is immediate and the meeting is harmonious. The same cannot be said for when members of different groups come in contact. Even at a few trees' distance the respective males are likely to engage in prolonged bouts of mutual threatening, with rushes through foliage, vigorous shaking and sometimes breaking of branches, and much vocalizing with peculiar barking sounds. They may also smear branches with secretions from special scent glands on the chest.

Howler monkey troops exhibit similar aggression on the occasions when they meet face-to-face, with much commotion and even direct fighting, but since such squabbles are so taxing, like many monkeys they do their best to avoid close contact. Howler troops keep apart in the forest by listening to one another's extremely penetrating calls (see Howls and Hoots, page 1422). Squirrel monkey groups also try to avoid one another, but since they are not territorial the ranges of neighboring groups overlap and groups often meet. In these monkeys, however, tolerance is the order of the day, and two groups may even feed close together in the same fruiting tree without reacting aggressively.

Group life has obvious social and reproductive attractions for communicative, polygamous monkeys, and it can also bring advantages in terms of food and security. A large group working together is better able to locate prime food sources such as trees with fruit coming into season, as well as having more chance of defending those sources from competing groups. For capuchins, squirrel monkeys, and other species that are frequently attacked by large birds of prey, the larger the group the more chance that at least one individual will spot an incoming predator in time to raise the alarm with a sharp call.

GROUP DISADVANTAGES

But group life can be difficult too, especially for subordinate animals in the group hierarchy. Those adult males and adult females that have established higher status in the group, largely because they can best hold their own in confrontations, usually have

HOWLS AND HOOTS

Monkeys are responsible for many of the most distinctive calls of the tropical forest, none more so than the howler and night monkeys.

Troops of howler monkeys engage in bouts of calling early each morning, from time to time at night, and regularly while out foraging to advertise their presence to neighboring troops and so insure that groups remain discretely spaced. The dawn chorus produced by these monkeys is one of the most bizarre sounds in nature. Howler monkeys possess an enlarged bone in the throat, the hyoid, which acts as a resonator and amplifier when air is expelled through its cavity. The sound that results is reminiscent of the roar of a big cat, only much more prolonged and earsplitting at close range. It is so loud that it can carry up to two miles (three kilometers) across the canopy, and since the entire group commonly call in unison, their rising and falling notes combine from afar to sound like the roar of distant wind. When one group stops, another elsewhere inevitably takes up the chorus.

The call of a night monkey is a series of short, mournful hoots, which, though low in tone, can easily carry for a quarter of a mile (400 m). Only the male calls, either to announce his presence to potential mates or to stake a claim on a territory.

better access to prime feeding sites. Subordinates may be forced to the periphery of the group and only allowed to feed when others have passed on. In the brown capuchin monkey, for example, a heightening of confrontations when food is scarce may even force the subordinates to strike out in small groups or on their own.

Those species that live in small, monogamous groups seem either to concentrate on food that is small in size and naturally scattered through the habitat or live in such a way that they are at reduced risk from predators. Either factor takes away a key advantage of group life. Titi monkeys, for example, rely largely on fruit from small, scattered fruit trees that could not sustain many monkeys and which the little groups find by systematically foraging through their small home ranges every few days. Night monkeys tend to feed in individual trees with plentiful food, but since they are nocturnal and eagles are

Night monkey groups are small, consisting of an adult pair plus one or two offspring.

Ken Lucas/Planet Earth Pictures

diurnal they do not require the safety in numbers of a large group.

Along with the sakis, titi monkeys and night monkeys live in tight family groups consisting of an adult pair and up to three immature offspring from consecutive years. Subadult young have to leave the family group and both adults are antagonistic toward neighbors of their own sex. The adults maintain their exclusive pair bond from one year to the next and lead their young around small home ranges from 1.2–25 acres (0.5 to 10 hectares) in area. Titi monkeys and night monkeys are renowned for their long bouts of dawn calling, which help different groups space themselves out across the forest at respectful distances. In the titi, such calls carry for as much as 2,300 ft (700 m). For the rest of the day, however, titis tend to move and feed as silently as possible, to avoid attracting the attention of hawks.

GROOMING

Titi monkeys strengthen the bond between group members with attentive interaction, especially during rest periods when grooming is common. The male titi is renowned for the degree of devotion he lavishes upon his offspring. He both carries and grooms his infant with as much tenderness as a mother. Yellow-handed titis, which all sleep together on a single bough, indulge in a final bout of grooming before settling down for the night.

Social interaction, however, is by no means confined to monogamous species. Ouakaris are also avid groomers, luxuriating in the valuable attention their long fur receives. A monkey soliciting grooming from a companion will typically come and lie alongside in a posture that signals its desire. The other will then spend several minutes picking through the fur to remove pests and debris—especially from the head and upper back, which are not easy for an animal to reach. Then the roles are reversed.

Interaction between groups and between individuals within a large group, as we have seen, can also be aggressive. As well as the thrashing about, branch waving, and calling employed to ward off territorial intruders and intimidate reproductive or hierarchical rivals, cebid monkeys have a typical threat expression of open mouth and bared canines. Night monkeys even show various aggressive postures visible to dark-adapted eyes, including an arching of the back, bristling of the hairs, and stiff-legged jumps. ■

TITI TANGLERS

Titis have the curious and delightful habit of entwining their tails when resting on a bough (above). *No other primate is known to do this.*

Illustration Evi Antoniou

LIFE CYCLE

The social patterns of cebid monkeys strongly influence their reproductive and developmental behavior. At the most basic level, small-group species maintain pair bonds and the young are looked after to some extent by both parents. Larger-group species, on the other hand, are more

SOCIAL ADVANCEMENT

Soon the offspring starts to climb and explore on its own, making contact with other members of the troop and making "friends" among both young and old (left).

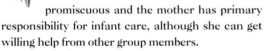

promiscuous and the mother has primary responsibility for infant care, although she can get willing help from other group members.

Courtship is a slower, more involved affair among monogamous monkeys than it is among those species that do not establish lasting pair bonds. A newly forming pair of titi monkeys may spend many days examining and sniffing one another, sitting close together, grooming and entwining tails before mating. In capuchins and howlers, courtship is brief and to the point. A female approaches a group male, or occasionally one from a neighboring troop, and makes mouth gestures to which he replies in kind if interested. They then mate and soon after separate. A female woolly spider monkey announces her readiness to mate with special calls, attracting any number of males with whom she may mate.

Gestation in cebid monkeys lasts from four to seven months, and births take place in the trees. Only very rarely are twins born. The newborn infant immediately clings to its mother's fur, quickly finding for itself the most secure site on which to be carried, which may be on the back, the belly, or in the groin. Several weeks may ensue before the tiny youngster is ready to clamber off the mother when she rests, and tentatively take hold of the branch or clamber onto another body in the troop.

Illustration Joanne Cowne

Development of young is generally more prolonged in the larger species. A young titi is weaned at about five months and may be sexually mature in three years, while a young male howler is nursed for eighteen months and may not reach maturity until its eighth year.

Older siblings as well as parents are allowed to handle and groom infant titis, night monkeys, and sakis at least after the first weeks of life, but it is the young of polygamous species that tend to have the most varied social interaction. Female companions of a mother squirrel monkey help care for and carry an infant while she forages. By its seventh month, a

AT TWO MONTHS

of age the infant is more active, regularly clambering off its mother and onto siblings who come to help. At this stage the youngster is carried lengthwise (above).

GROWING UP

The life of a young brown capuchin

MATING

...n the brown capuchin is ...nitiated by the female, who ...estures and calls to a male with ...yebrows raised (above). *After a ...eriod of close physical ...ontact, they mate.*

Adrian Warren/Ardea

PIGGYBACK

For the first month of its life, an infant capuchin clings across its mother's back, seldom moving from this position except when ready to be suckled (left).

Sakis live in small family groups, in which the female is responsible for rearing the young.

young ouakari may still be dependent on its mother, but nevertheless spends much time playing with other monkeys and is sometimes carried by males.

In its early years, a monkey seems to have plenty to learn. Much of the behavior it will employ in adult life to find food and shelter, move through the trees, react to danger, assert itself socially, and find a mate appears to be acquired rather than innate. Some of the learning comes from exploration of its immediate surroundings, while a great deal of the rest comes from play—not just with peers in the group but also with older animals. ■

in SIGHT

FATHER CARE

Males of many monkey species take an interest in their young, but in titi family groups the father takes primary responsibility for caring for the youngest offspring. An infant titi spends more time in paternal care than with either its mother or its siblings. It is the father that usually carries the infant unless it is being suckled, and after nursing the youngster soon starts to cry out for him again. He grooms it most readily and rushes to protect it when heavy rain falls, high winds blow, or any other danger threatens.

FROM BIRTH TO DEATH

BROWN CAPUCHIN

BREEDING: NONSEASONAL, ALTHOUGH BIRTH PEAKS MAY OCCUR IN RAINY SEASON	**WEIGHT AT BIRTH:** 9–10 OZ (250–290 G)
GESTATION: 150–160 DAYS	**FIRST SOLID FOOD:** 2 MONTHS
LITTER SIZE: 1	**WEANING:** 6–11 MONTHS
LITTER FREQUENCY: USUALLY ONCE EVERY 2 YEARS	**SEXUAL MATURITY:** 2–6 YEARS
	LONGEVITY: UP TO 40 YEARS IN CAPTIVITY

NEW WORLD, OLD THREAT

VIRTUALLY WITHOUT EXCEPTION, CEBID MONKEYS ARE ON THE DECLINE AS GROWING HUMAN POPULATIONS ENCROACH ON THEIR FOREST HOMES; SOME ARE ALREADY AT THE BRINK OF EXTINCTION

For all their diversity and adaptability, cebid monkeys across the American tropics face enormous hurdles simply surviving in a world increasingly dominated by human beings, their fellow primates. The story of their plight is a familiar mixture of habitat destruction, overhunting, and excessive capture of live animals, in many cases brought about by people who themselves face tremendous economic pressures. As a result, all cebids are under some degree of threat, although the seriousness of the problem varies greatly from species to species and from region to region.

At the genus level, the most endangered monkeys are the woolly monkeys, the spider monkeys, and, most of all, the woolly spider monkey. All these large animals are under severe pressures almost wherever they occur. In terms of biodiversity, a genus that is threatened wholesale is arguably of more conservation concern than a threatened species because it represents something still more unique in nature. If that genus dies out, an entire type of animal becomes lost forever. The argument applies equally to a "monotypic" genus or one that contains just a single species—such as the woolly spider monkey—because again there is nothing else quite like it.

SHOT FOR THE POT

Woolly monkeys and spider monkeys are highly vulnerable for several reasons. As animals that live and gain their fruit food from the high canopy of mature rain forests, they are sensitive to any disturbance or degradation of their habitat. They are commonly shot for food because of their large size and their especially flavorsome meat, and their young have long been in demand as pets, especially young common woolly monkeys, which are probably the most popular species. Delayed maturity and low rates of breeding in these monkeys compound the problems by hampering any chance a local population might have to recover from such depredations. Spider monkeys will survive in partially altered habitat, but depend upon

Squirrel monkeys (below) *are smaller, and hence more adaptable, than other cebid monkeys.*

Francois Gohier/Ardea

The irresistible charm of a young smoky woolly monkey (right) *is, partly, the cause of its rarity.*

Adrian Warren/Ardea

THEN & NOW

This map shows how the forests of Central America have been destroyed in recent years.

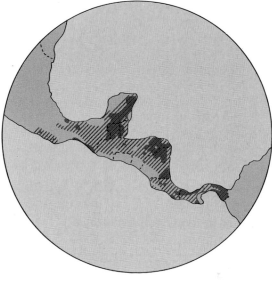

BEFORE   **NOW**

Outside protected areas, the future for forest animals in Central America is fragile indeed. Already, the Central American squirrel monkey is considered endangered. Others under severe threat in all or part of their ranges include the Guatemalan howler, the mantled howler, and the black-handed spider monkey.

The forests in which these species live are among the most threatened in the world. From central Mexico to Panama, huge swaths of land have been stripped of trees to make way for farming, plantations, and ranching and to provide wood for fuel and the timber trade. Less than two-fifths of Central America's original forested area still has trees, and of this much has been degraded by logging or broken up into patches by small-scale land clearance. This is one of the most densely settled regions of the Americas, with an average 115 people per sq mile (300 per sq km). Given that much of the lowland area is taken up by industrial-scale ranching and agriculture, the expanding numbers of landless poor are forced to clear new plots in upland forests where slopes are steep and the soil poor and easily eroded. Such plots may have to be abandoned and new ones cleared every few years.

extensive patches of tall gallery forest. Not surprisingly, when people begin to settle in a new part of the western Amazon, it is generally black spider monkeys and common woolly monkeys that are the first species to dwindle and then disappear from the surrounding area. Hence these monkeys are now largely restricted in the wild to remote, virgin forest.

Smaller monkeys with less specialized habitat requirements and that yield little meat tend to be in a better position. Squirrel monkeys and night monkeys, for example, remain in fairly healthy numbers across much of South America. Yet in certain areas, particularly those that have been heavily deforested, they too have suffered dramatic decline

NIGHT MONKEYS HAVE, IN THE PAST, BEEN COLLECTED FOR THE PET TRADE AND FOR BIOMEDICAL RESEARCH

as their habitat has been taken away. Night monkeys, like many of their kind, respond poorly to attempts at captive breeding. Success depends on keeping only mated pairs together, for with any other social combination the individuals suffer from stress and even physical injury.

Titi monkeys often undergo similar problems in captivity. Researchers in Germany recently found that individuals would slowly sicken and eventually die through no obvious cause. When such an invalid was removed from the oppressive company of other titis and placed in solitary conditions, its health was restored almost overnight.

DEFORESTATION

Habitat disruption in the tropical forests takes many forms. Often it begins when a new dirt road is cut through previously virgin territory, perhaps to link distant towns or to service mines, dams, and other developments. Settlers, many of them desperate for land, quickly colonize the roadside, cutting and burning clearings. Side roads are cut, and the colonization process spreads out. In other situations, large tracts of forest are taken up with ranching or logging. Though logging may not require wholesale clearance of the forest in the way that ranching demands, even the selective removal of valuable timber trees breaks up the canopy and destroys much of the ground vegetation. Forests around settlements may also be degraded if not destroyed by timber extraction for firewood.

Squirrel monkeys can survive outside mature, intact forests, but they cannot survive where the forest has been so thinned out that only scant tree or shrub cover remains. This is the case across

Nick Gordon/Ardea

ENDANGERED SPECIES

LAST STAND OF THE MURIQUI

The woolly spider monkey, or muriqui as it is known locally, has two main distinctions among the American monkeys. It is the largest species; and it is the most critically endangered of them all. Only about 300 individuals are thought to remain in the wild and these form small populations scattered over three different Brazilian states. This animal finds itself in such a critical situation because of centuries of relentless forest clearance and intensive hunting. It simply lives in the wrong place.

The muriqui is endemic to the Atlantic Forest ecosystem of southeast Brazil—a once-vast rain-forest habitat so depleted and fragmented now that no fewer than fourteen of the twenty-one types of monkey that occur there are regarded as endangered. Their home has been steadily cut, dug, and burned away ever since European settlers started to arrive in this part of Brazil in the 16th century. In the ensuing centuries, most of the country's farms, plantations, settlements, roads, mines, industry, and, of course, people became concentrated in the Atlantic Forest region, particularly in the very heart of the muriqui's range in the states of Sao Paulo, Rio de Janeiro, Espirito Santo, and Minas Gerais.

Less than five percent of the original Atlantic Forest now remains, most of it in reserves or in small, fragmented patches on private farms and ranches. But for the muriqui, the problem has not just been loss

CONSERVATION MEASURES

● In 1975 the United States Department of Health, Education and Welfare effectively banned the importation of primates into the United States for sale as pets; it also imposed severe limitations upon importation for other uses.

● The following cebid monkeys are currently listed in Appendix I of CITES, the Convention on International Trade in Endangered Species: the red-backed squirrel monkey; mantled howler; white-nosed bearded saki; bald

home. Surrounded by a burgeoning
ral population this big monkey has been
avily hunted for its flesh, so that even
ere it has a forest fragment in which to
e it remains at risk from poachers.

The monkey was such rewarding quarry
at early European explorers came to rely
the animal as a source of meat during
eir travels. But at that time the vast forests
ntained an estimated 400,000 woolly spi-
r monkeys. Today the species is on the
ink of extinction. About 150 of the surviv-
g muriqui occur in areas of intact forest
ithin two ranches, one in Sao Paulo state,
e other in Minas Gerais. The others are
spersed across eight different locations,
ch of these places holding groups of
tween five and twenty-five individuals.

Andrew Young/Oxford Scientific Films

THE WOOLLY SPIDER MONKEY IS THE MOST
ENDANGERED OF THE CEBID MONKEYS.

uakari and black-headed ouakari;
ellow-tailed woolly monkey;
oth subspecies of the black-
anded spider monkey, and the
oolly spider monkey. CITES
ppendix I, the Convention's
aximum protection category,
ipulates that the listed
ecies or subspecies may
ot be exported for
ommercial purposes
om the country of
rigin without special
spensation.

most of the range of the Central American squirrel
monkey in Costa Rica and Panama, where the
conversion of land for cattle ranches, banana plantations, and sugar cane and rice cultivation has put
this species in critical danger. Probably few more
than 3,000 survive.

TRAPPING

Here and elsewhere, the case of squirrel monkeys
also illustrates the strains that excessive capture of
live monkeys can place on wild populations. The
pet trade still threatens surviving populations of
Central American squirrel monkeys, and, in the
past, so many squirrel monkeys were taken from
more accessible parts of Colombia and Peru for
captive export that the trade began to run out of
supply. Between 1968 and 1972 alone over
170,000 squirrel monkeys were imported into the
United States, a large proportion of which were
destined for biomedical research laboratories.

Today, the bulk of the trade for cebid monkeys is
local. All over South America, monkeys are popular pets and most species suffer some degree of
commercial capture. The effects on wild populations
are not always severe but they are worsened by high
mortality levels in the trade. Capturing an infant
normally requires the mother and other protective
members of the troop to be shot first. Often the
method is to shoot a mother from the trees and pick
off the infant still clinging to her fur. Many infants, of
course, die from the fall, and many others perish
from the traumas of capture, poor transport conditions, and inadequate care before they are sold.

Infant mortality through natural causes is a
pressing problem for many species. Field research

suggests that some four-fifths of young red howler monkeys survive their first year, but also that nearly 50 percent of infant deaths result from infanticide by older males.

Those monkey species or subspecies that are naturally restricted in range or naturally scarce are particularly vulnerable in conservation terms. Excessive human pressure on their populations can quickly send them close to extinction. The yellow-tailed woolly monkey, which occupies a restricted range in the cloud forest of Peru, is a prime example. Only rediscovered in its rugged terrain in 1974, nearly half a century after it was last reported, this species is already beset by forest clearance and hunting following the opening up of new roads.

The bald ouakari is legally protected from capture and export, but unfortunately its rain-forest habitat is, like much of the Amazon, up for grabs. Soon this spectacular primate may be gone for good.

J. Sauvanel/Oxford Scientific Films

ALONGSIDE MAN

MONKEY BUSINESS

The tradition of keeping monkeys as pets has a long history in South America. Captive monkeys taken from the wild, often when young, are still a common sight in indigenous and rural settlements and are sold for cash in urban markets, even though such trade may be technically illegal. At an early stage in colonial history some monkeys also became sought-after pets overseas, none more so than capuchins. It is partly because so many capuchins ended up as pets in Europe that these monkeys so typify the popular conception of what monkeys look and act like. Active, agile, intelligent, and curious, these are the species traditionally associated with street performers and organ-grinders. They became popular pets and exhibits in menageries not just because of their entertainment value but because they are among the most hardy of species and can best tolerate the climatic discomforts of life away from home.

The ouakaris, although they occupy larger ranges, are also quite restricted in their preference for flooded forest habitats and are naturally quite low in number. The parts of the Amazon Basin in which they reside are relatively little affected by habitat modification, but since they are riverside habitats access to them is possible from distant settlements and the monkeys are easy to kill. Black ouakaris and a race of the bald ouakari, the red ouakari, have been heavily hunted for their meat in Colombia and Peru respectively. Their flesh is so highly prized that it has been the main reason for their decline.

The ability of hunters to penetrate deep into forest is one reason why monkeys tend to disappear quickly from around newly settled "frontier" settlements, even when the forest itself remains largely intact. As in tropical West Africa, for many rural people monkey meat can be an important source of protein in the diet, and monkeys are often shot illegally to feed workers at remote construction sites or logging and mining camps. A few monkeys, including the bearded saki, are even taken as bait for attracting fur-bearing cats such as the jaguar. As in so many cases like this, it is not easy for developed nations to force their own ideals on countries where the needs of resident wild animals are given a far lower priority than those of local people. ∎

INTO THE FUTURE

With at least twenty entire species and certain races of a further eight species already threatened, the cebid monkeys have a drastic need for effective conservation. Few populations of monkeys anywhere in the Americas have their future assured, given their dependence on forest vegetation and the current pressures on their habitat.

Maintaining existing protected areas and creating new reserves is likely to be the key to their survival. Large national parks and smaller biological reserves already exist in many forested regions, notably in the Amazonian and Atlantic Forest zones of Brazil, in eastern Peru, Colombia, Venezuela, Costa Rica, and Belize. But often they are too poorly funded for reserve staff to prevent incursions from farmers and hunters. In some cases national park authorities have even allowed logging operations within park boundaries. There is also a pressing need for new

PREDICTION

A PRECARIOUS HABITAT

Efforts to conserve individual species, combined with the refuges provided for wildlife in general across tropical America, have already proved vital for saving rare monkeys. But the likelihood is that more animals will face problems in the future as inroads into their habitat widen.

refuges to be designated, in some cases in collaboration with private landowners, for key species.

Protection of habitats is backed up by efforts to protect individual species themselves from hunting and persecution. International laws such as CITES, and national laws passed by Brazil, Mexico, Peru, and Colombia, have helped to stem poaching and control the export of live animals, but there are endless instances when such laws are flouted. Arguably more important are efforts to raise public awareness and support for monkey conservation. For both the woolly spider monkey and the yellow-tailed woolly monkey, major education campaigns have taken place in Brazil and Peru. Focusing on those communities that live in the vicinity of these monkeys' refuges, conservationists have provided lecture programs, films, museum exhibits, school materials, posters, stickers, and T-shirts, all emphasizing the need to protect the animals and their fragile habitats. The woolly spider monkey has even been depicted on Brazilian postage stamps. ■

Illustration Peter Beresford/Wildlife Art Agency

INTERNATIONAL HELP

Cebid monkeys are bred in zoos around the world, and careful monitoring of the captive stock may be important in the future for some of the critically endangered species and subspecies.

Several large conservation agencies also support the monkeys. The International Union for the Conservation of Nature (IUCN), or the World Conservation Union, for example, has been formulating and coordinating Action Plans for Primate Conservation, one of which is devoted to tropical America. The Plan covers practical monkey conservation projects, as well as training and education efforts for conservation staff from the countries concerned. The World Wide Fund for Nature (WWF) has been very active within this plan. It has helped, for example, to fund the campaigns for the yellow-tailed woolly monkey and the muriqui, and is undertaking research into the status and ecological needs of monkeys in the wild.

COLOBINE MONKEYS

Colobine monkeys belong t
the Old World monkey famil
Cercopithecoidae, within th
primate order. Other mem
bers of the family include:

GUENONS

MACAQUES

BABOONS

MANDRILLS

MANGABEYS

Javed Jafferji/Oxford Scientific Films

CLASSIFICATION

The monkeys in this article comprise the subfamily Colobinae, within the Old World monkey family, Cercopithecidae.

ORDER

Primates

FAMILY

Cercopithecidae

SUBFAMILY

Colobinae

GENERA

Colobus
(pied colobus monkeys)

Procolobus
(olive colobus monkeys)

Piliocolobus
(red colobus monkeys)

Rhinopithecus
(snub-nosed langurs)

Nasalis
(proboscis monkeys)

Trachypithecus
(brow-ridged langurs)

Simias
(pig-tailed langur)

Pygathrix
(douc langurs)

Presbytis
(leaf-monkey langurs)

Semnopithecus
(Hanuman langur)

FRIENDS IN HIGH PLACES

THE COLOBINE MONKEYS HAVE THE EDGE OVER OTHER OLD WORLD MONKEY SPECIES IN THAT THEIR BROAD, LEAF-BASED DIET GIVES THEM FULL RANGE OF THE MANY DIFFERENT FORESTS OF THE WORLD

The large family Cercopithecidae (serk-o-pith-ECK-id-ie) is one of the most diverse groups of primates: Its members display a wealth of rich and dazzling coat patterns and colors; of beards, mustaches, shoulder patches, and tail tufts, and their collective diet includes anything from insects and fruit to tobacco plants.

The cercopithecids are widespread over the "Old World" of Africa and Eurasia, so they are called the Old World monkeys. Their counterparts in the "New World" of the Americas are extremely distant cousins. The two groups, now separated by the Atlantic, derive from common ancestors that lived some 30–40 million years ago, before the Americas drifted away from the great landmasses. The American or New World monkeys took to the trees of the warm, moist rain forests, developing a useful gripping tail to serve as a fifth limb, while those in the Old World

The curious-looking male proboscis monkey (below) is a native of the mangrove swamps of Borneo.

Rod Williams/Bruce Coleman Ltd.

diversified to occupy habitats both on solid ground and up aloft among the branches.

OLD WORLD SUBFAMILIES

The Old World monkeys defy simple generalizations, but they do fall into two broad camps and as such have been divided into two subfamilies.

The Cercopithecinae (serk-o-pith-EK-in-ie) contains sixteen species and includes the drills, macaques, mangabeys, guenons, and baboons. They are often stocky, well-built monkeys as they spend a fair amount of time on the ground in savanna and open woodland and eat a broad diet, and many species live in groups with rigorous pecking orders.

The Colobinae (col-o-BEEN-ie), the subjects of

As in many colobine species, female langurs take turns to hold a newborn infant.

Martin Harvey/NHPA

ISLAND RELICS

Some colobine species or races, such as the Zanzibar red colobus and the Mentawai Islands sureli (soo-RAY-lee), found their way onto islands. Living on an island can play havoc with an animal's evolution: It can slow it down or speed it up, depending on the compatibility of that animal to the local ecosystem. The Zanzibar red colobus, imprisoned on its own luxury fortress off the coast of Tanzania, southeast Africa, has coat colors and patterns that betray connections with other races of colobus far inland. Which race came first? It could simply be an island aberration, but some zoologists believe that the Zanzibar red colobus is an ancient relic representing the stock from which all colobuses evolved.

this volume, comprise thirty-seven species and are more or less the opposite. Lean and lithe, they are superbly acrobatic and live mainly in the forests of Africa and Asia—and therefore they tend to eat more leaves than anything else—and, while far from solitary, they often have looser social structures than those of the cercopithecines.

There are several physical traits, too, which zoologists use to distinguish between the two subfamilies. Perhaps most importantly, the colobines lack cheek pouches but instead have large salivary glands and a complex, multichambered stomach, while the cercopithecines do have cheek pouches but possess a much more simple stomach. These anatomical differences are intimately bound up with the monkeys' environments and daily habits.

ORIGINS

The colobines can be traced back tentatively to an origin in Africa, through fossils dating from 30–40 million years ago. They were probably forest-dwellers that had started to specialize in eating leaves, while their cercopithecine cousins developed a preference for fruit.

The colobines spread widely through what is now Europe and Asia, when the world was warmer and moist, tropical forests were more widespread. Indeed, the colobines once ranged from sites as far afield as England and China—but in particular, they settled happily and diversified in the forests of India, Malaysia, Vietnam, China, Borneo, and many other Asian countries. Africa, too, hosted several colobine species—many more than survive there today; the now-extinct colobines probably died out through competition with other monkeys.

During climatic changes about 20 million years ago, the world's forests retreated toward the equator and dryland barriers effectively separated the African and the Asian branches of the colobine subfamily. Today there are some twenty-seven colobine species in Asia and eleven in Africa, and in terms of evolutionary advancement they remain some of the most primitive living monkeys.

THE COLOBINES

The subfamily Colobinae contains up to ten genera, although some zoologists dispute this number and would rather list only six. Africa is home to three genera: *Colobus* (COL-o-buss), which contains the black colobus monkeys, *Procolobus* (PRO-col-o-buss), the olive colobus genus, and *Piliocolobus* (PILL-ee-o-colobuss), the red colobus genus. The other seven genera are found in Asia, and comprise langurs, leaf monkeys, and the so-called "odd-nosed" monkeys—doucs, snub-nosed monkeys, and the proboscis monkey.

A peculiarity of the colobines is a distinctly small thumb. The length of the thumb varies according to the species; proportionately longest in the snub-nosed and proboscis monkeys, it appears only as a tiny button in the colobus monkeys. The word *kolobos* actually means "shortened" or "mutilated" in the Greek language. But colobuses do not really need their thumb, since they can swing skillfully through the trees using their hooked fingers and their leafy diet does not require too much manual dexterity. ■

THE COLOBINE'S FAMILY TREE

The family Cercopithecidae of Old World monkeys comprises two subfamilies: the Colobinae and the Cercopithecinae. Zoologists still debate the naming of certain colobine genera and the placement of species within them. For example, the Hanuman langur is sometimes included in the Presbytis, *rather than the* Semnopithecus, *genus.*

COLOBUS MONKEY

Colobus (*COL-o-buss*)

Procolobus (*pro-COL-o-buss*)

The colobus monkeys of Africa are generally slender, with a long tail and a calloused rump. With the exception of the satanic black colobus, the black colobus monkeys of the genus Colobus have varying patterns of bold black-and-white markings on a glossy black coat. The red and olive colobuses of the genus Procolobus are marked with warm reddish and cool greenish colors respectively.

BROW-RIDGED & HANUMAN LANGURS

Semnopithecus (*sem-no-PITH-eck-uss*)

Trachypithecus (*track-ee-PITH-eck-uss*)

The langurs and leaf monkeys of the genus Semnopithecus are, in general, vegetarian acrobats of the tree canopy. The best studied of these is the Hanuman langur (left). This smoky gray species with black face and hands is particularly common in India, where it is held in sacred esteem due to its fabled association with the Hindu monkey god, Hanuman.

Color illustrations Steve Kingston. B/W illustrations Ruth Grewcock

OLD WORLD MONKEYS

SURELI
Presbytis
(PREZ–bit–is)

The six species of sureli are found in the forests of Borneo, Sumatra, the Malay Peninsula, and nearby islands. Like the leaf monkeys, most surelis are descriptively named: They are the grizzled, maroon, mitered, pale-thighed, banded, and Mentawai Islands surelis.

SNUB-NOSED MONKEY
Rhinopithecus
(rie-no-PITH-eck-uss)

The snub-nosed monkeys of the genus Rhinopithecus live in China and Southeast Asia, and include some of the rarest and most richly colored of all primates. Although rare, China's golden snub-nosed monkey (right) has strongholds in remote mountain forests.

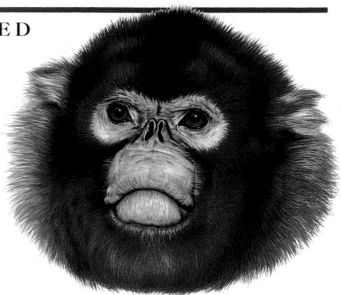

PROBOSCIS MONKEY
Nasalis larvatis
(nah-SAH-liss lar-VAH-tiss)

This unforgettable inmate of the mangrove forests is best known for the long, pendulous and cartoonish nose of the adult male—but it is also unusual for its social behavior, which is more typical of ground-dwelling monkeys.

SUBFAMILY
CERCOPITHECINAE

MACAQUES

GUENONS

MANGABEYS

BABOONS

ANATOMY: THE RED COLOBUS

The Hanuman langur (above left) measures 16–31 in (41–78 cm) from head to rump, and has a tail length of 27–42.5 in (69–108 cm). The olive colobus (above right) has a head-and-body length of 17–19.5 in (43–49 cm) and a tail length of 22.5–25 in (57–64 cm).

THE FACE

bears the downward-pointing nostrils that are typical of the Old World monkeys, and there is a pronounced ridge framing the eyes. It is near naked, to enable full facial expression of moods and emotions.

PROBOSCIS MONKEY

GOLDEN LEAF MONKEY

HANUMAN MONKEY

Collectively, the colobines can boast a sumptuous array of finery in the form of coats, colors, and hairstyles. One of them alone has a face that suggests one of nature's practical jokes: the proboscis monkey.

THE LIMBS

are lean, but powerful muscles on the hind legs enable long leaps across gaps in the trees. Nevertheless, although the red colobus can stand erect, it travels on all fours and is a surprisingly clumsy climber.

SKELETON

The colobus's long muscle fibers and elastic ligaments are stretched over a light, long-boned and loose-jointed frame. Hands and feet are fine-boned for added dexterity, and, like most primates, the colobus can rotate the two forearm bones (the radius and ulna) about each other to aid hand-over-hand movement through the branches.

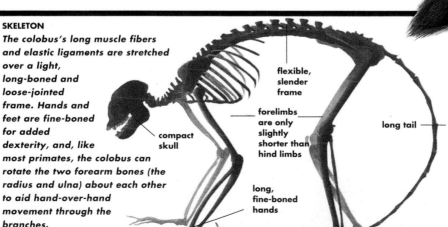

compact skull

flexible, slender frame

forelimbs are only slightly shorter than hind limbs

long, fine-boned hands

long tail

COLOBUS HAND

The hands have four long, fine digits and a shortened thumb, each having a fingernail. In the case of the colobus monkeys, however, the thumb may be absent altogether or reduced to a small button bearing only a rudimentary nail.

LANGU HAND

X-ray illustrations Elisabeth Smith

HAND **FOOT** **HAND** **FOOT**

COLOBUS MONKEY **LANGUR MONKEY**

Like all primates, colobines have long dexterous digits on both their hands and their feet, but what sets them apart from their other relatives is their shortened thumbs. The length of the thumb varies between the colobine species. In the case of the colobus monkeys the thumb is practically nonexistent—their leafy diet and arboreal lifestyle does not require too much dexterity.

THE STOMACH

often appears rather potbellied. This is simply because it is huge and contains many separate chambers. Special "waiting rooms" for the monkey's food contain bacteria that attack vegetation, fermenting and softening it before stomach acids get to work in the main chamber.

THE TAIL

is long and fine, unlike the flamboyant "brushes" of some pied colobus races. It is often held aloft in a social gesture to other troop members.

FACT FILE:

THE RED COLOBUS

CLASSIFICATION

GENUS: *PILIOCOLOBUS*

SPECIES: *BADIUS*

SIZE

HEAD–BODY LENGTH: 18.5–25 IN (47–63 CM)

TAIL LENGTH: 20.5–29.5 IN (52–75 CM)

WEIGHT: 12–22 LB (5.5–10 KG). BLACK COLOBUSES ARE ABOUT 10 PERCENT LARGER THAN REDS

COLORATION

VERY VARIABLE ACCORDING TO THE RACE

THE RED CONTENT VARIES FROM A FULL, RICH CHESTNUT BROWN BACK IN ONE RACE TO LITTLE MORE THAN A RUSTY BROWN CROWN IN ANOTHER

UNDERPARTS WHITE WITH A TINGE OF ORANGE, YELLOW, ORANGE-RED, OR CHESTNUT

UPPER PARTS GRAY, CHARCOAL, MOTTLED GRAY AND CREAM, CHESTNUT, OR GRAYISH BLACK

TAIL REDDISH BLACK OR GRAY

FEATURES

ARMS SLIGHTLY SHORTER THAN LEGS

GENITAL SWELLINGS VISIBLE IN ADULT FEMALE AND YOUNG MALE

FACIAL WHISKERS ARE USUALLY GRAY

MALE HAS A LARGER HEAD THAN FEMALE, COMPLETE WITH LARGER CANINE TEETH AND BEARD

ALMOST ALWAYS SEEN UP IN THE TREES, RARELY DESCENDING TO THE GROUND

MALE'S BUTTOCK CALLUSES ARE SEPARATED BY FURRED SKIN, UNLIKE MOST OTHER MALE COLOBINE SPECIES

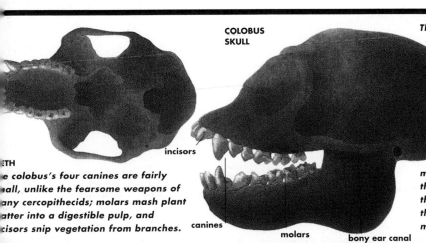

COLOBUS SKULL

LANGUR SKULL

incisors

canines

molars

bony ear canal

compact skull

...ETH

...e colobus's four canines are fairly ...all, unlike the fearsome weapons of ...any cercopithecids; molars mash plant ...atter into a digestible pulp, and ...cisors snip vegetation from branches.

The typical colobine skull (left and right) has a compact form, unlike the elongated, more doglike muzzle of cercopithecids such as drills and baboons. The male's head is larger, being equipped with more formidable jaw muscles. On the underside of the braincase can be seen the bony ear canals, features that are absent in New World monkeys and marmosets.

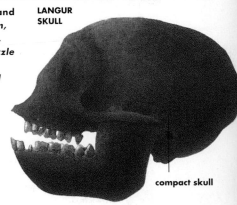

TREETOP TRAVELERS

WITH ONE OR TWO NOTABLE EXCEPTIONS, COLOBINES RARELY DESCEND TO THE GROUND. IT IS SAFER IN THE TREE CANOPY, WHERE FOOD IS WITHIN EASY REACH AND THE BOUGHS ARE READY MADE FOR SNOOZING

It is midafternoon, and a gentle, insistent wind ruffles the foliage of a forest on the steep slopes of a valley in Bhutan, filling the high green canopy with a powerful rustling like the hiss and roar of distant surf. Suddenly, a louder crash is heard as a monkey hurtles through the air, tail hung low and rusty orange limbs thrust to the fore, to make a perfect four-point landing on another branch across a small clearing. Further movement in the canopy catches the eye—there are several more richly furred acrobats up aloft, each waiting patiently in line for its turn to leap into the void: It is a troop of golden leaf monkeys, crisscrossing the aerial runways of its home range.

TRAPEZE ARTISTES

The golden leaf monkey is endowed with the breathtaking leaping skills that are the stock in trade of most colobines. That these monkeys are so agile is hardly surprising, for they have been honing their trapeze skills for millenia. While other primates took tentatively to a life on the ground—some even making the permanent upgrade to two-footed movement—the colobines have never really left the trees. There is no need, for they have all the food they need in the canopy, as well as a special type of stomach to process it. The dark arbors among the branches offer sites, too, for rest and shelter. And so, with one or two exceptions, colobines are seldom seen on the ground.

Not all colobines have equal agility, however. Although the red colobus can leap down to cross gaps of 66 ft (20 m) or more, using the natural bounce of its landing branch to rocket back up to the next destination, its galloping, squirrel-like mode of travel has been frankly described by one zoologist as "suicidal." Nor is it the only butter-fingers in the group: Proboscis monkeys, normally

cautious travelers, can easily fall to the ground and suffer injury when fleeing danger; proof of this lies in the many skeletons that have been found with fractured bones. But overall, there is no doubting the colobines' skills: The late Gerald Durrell witnessed pied colobuses making tremendous vertical leaps of more than 150 ft (45 m) from tree crowns to the understory with no apparent injury. The guereza, too, is a superb leaper, as are the langurs.

Slightly at odds with their acrobatics is the fact that, much more so than other monkeys, the colobines are fairly serene in their gestures and social habits. This placid nature is another by-product of their arboreal heritage. Ground-based monkeys, such as baboons, rely far more heavily on calls and expressive gestures when settling

Starin/Ardea

Konrad Wothe/Bruce Coleman Ltd.

Leaping langurs! A Nilgiri langur moves from tree to tree with the expertise of an acrobat.

breeding rights, claiming territories, and evading predators. The male mandrill, probably the most vividly colored of cercopithecine monkeys, has a snarl fixed forever upon his wrinkled muzzle, in order to issue a continuous deterrent to his equally threatening rivals nearby on the plains. The colobines, by contrast, cannot gain much by making faces at each other when all they can see most of the time is their neighbor's rump disappearing among the foliage. As a result of this, plus the abundant supply of leafy food all around, there is generally less bickering within the troop—much of it would be a waste of breath.

There are times, however, when quick reactions to a loud call can save lives—especially when predators are about. Colobine monkeys are active during the day, when there are plenty of enemies

MALE LANGURS KEEP AN EYE ON TROOP MEMBERS WHO WANDER TOO FAR AFIELD, AND CALL THEM IN IF NECESSARY

about in the form of big cats, snakes, and birds of prey, and many species are clearly aware that "forewarned is forearmed." So each day, while the young are playing under the watchful eye of a female, the adult males in a dusky langur troop fulfill their vital role as sentries. They often take to the highest branches for the best view, and warn the others of approaching enemies with a series of gentle whoops and ear-piercing shrieks.

Sentry duty—which also occurs among capped langurs, deep in the mixed forests of India—is taken a stage further by the male banded leaf monkey. Upon spotting danger—for example, the broad wings of an eagle flitting through the dappled canopy—the sentry not only cries out to the troop but also tries to lure the big bird toward him, leaping out of range as it swoops nearer. The females and youngsters, meanwhile, crouch stock-still and silent until the danger is past.

Milder threats, such as a sudden downpour, will still cause a reaction. Like many colobines, Phayre's langur enjoys a quiet siesta in the noonday sun, but the first drops of rain will send it into the thick of the forest canopy to crouch upon a branch until all is clear again. Indeed, few colobines enjoy getting wet, although they can swim well if pushed. The only colobine that clearly relishes water is the proboscis monkey: It regularly takes to the network of rivers and streams among the mangrove forests.   ■

The Guinea forest red colobus is found in West Africa from Senegal to southwest Ghana.

HABITATS

Having evolved predominantly as leaf-eating experts, the colobines have spread out to occupy a range of forested and open habitats so completely diverse as to defy any generalization. Taking the subfamily as a whole, they can be found in forests ranging from coastal mangroves and lowland tropical rain forests to dry, deciduous montane woodlands, but will also break the colobine mold where it suits them, venturing into savanna and semidesert regions and even snow-bound mountain ranges.

Much of this diversity stems from dietary flexibility—or from its flip side: dietary specialization. An unfussy feeder like the Hanuman langur can exploit all manner of different environments; this species ranges from desert borders to moist tropical forest and alpine scrub, including many different environments in between, from sea level to altitudes of 13,123 ft (4,000 m) or more.

Other species, such as the satanic colobus population in the Sanaga River delta in Cameroon, are almost literally imprisoned by their food sources. The acidic sand dunes beside the Sanaga yield few nutrients to the local ebony forests, so the trees deploy poisonous chemicals—mainly tannins—in their leaves to deter leaf-eaters and so preserve their precious foliage. Not to be outdone, the satanic colobus has simply changed its diet to

Jean-Pierre Zwaenepoel/Bruce Colman Ltd.

FOCUS ON

COLOBINES IN VIETNAM

Vietnam, which forms much of the western coast of the South China Sea, is characterized by a long, narrow coastal plain topped and tailed by two large river deltas: the Red River and the Mekong River. Strung along the inland flank of the central coastal strip is the Chaîne Annamitique—a high mountain range with few passes. The heavy seasonal rains, year-round warmth, and diverse soil types have resulted in abundant growth of a wide variety of vegetation, including the lush rain forests that are home to colobines, in particular the Tonkin snub-nosed monkey, the doucs, and four leaf monkeys.

Terry Whittaker/Frank Lane Picture Agency

KEY

NASALIS MONKEYS

PYGATHRIX MONKEYS

PRESBYTIS & SEMNOPITHECUS MONKEYS

PROCOLOBUS MONKEYS

COLOBUS MONKEYS

eat the more agreeable seeds of the forest. This monkey is, however, geographically hemmed in on three sides by other colobus species, and if it moved out it might not cope easily with the competition for food or space. Likewise, the surrounding colobus species cannot move into this forest until they adapt their diet.

Dietary differences also come into play in the case of red and pied colobuses. The various forms of red colobus occupy the tropical forest belt around the "waist" of Africa, from Senegal east to the Rift Valley, and the closely related olive colobus is found only in a limited area of West Africa. The pied colobuses, however, not only overlap heavily with the reds' range in the tropics, but are also found right across to the east, as far as Ethiopia, in zones ranging from rain forest and bamboo thicket, semi-open woodland and riverside gallery forest, to arid woodlands with prolonged dry seasons. The reason for the ecological separation between red and pied colobuses lies largely in the fact that, while the red species go to great lengths to find succulent leaf

Hanuman, or common, langurs in India, huddling together during a downpour.

parts and fruits from several different plants, the pied colobuses can cope with much tougher leaves. The latter monkeys can therefore exploit habitats where, for example, all of their food sources lie in just one or two tree species. This situation partly mirrors that in Asia, where the widespread Hanuman langur can cope with a far wider diet than, for example, Biet's snub-nosed monkey, which eats only the needles of conifer trees in the Yun-ling Mountains of China and Tibet.

Many of the Asian colobines are, like the colobuses, denizens of lush rain forests, and until the mass deforestation of Southeast Asia they were spoiled for choice. The forests of that region—such as they survive—are among the world's most productive environments. Equatorial rain forests are famously rich in plant and animal life, due to their incredibly high rainfall and year-round constant temperature.

Vietnam is rich in colobines, but the leafy island of Borneo holds the record quota of species, with the proboscis monkey, four species of sureli, and the silvered leaf monkey. In terms of habitat, the proboscis monkey is one of the more unusual colobines: It can be found only in the coastal, riverside, and estuarine mangrove swamps, or mangals. ■

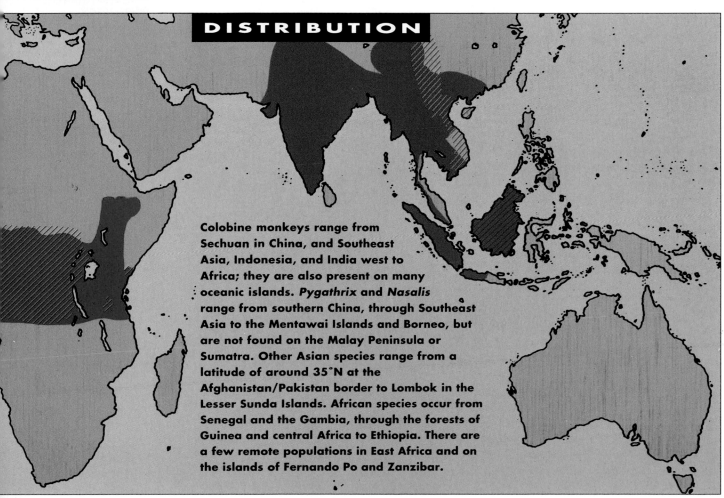

DISTRIBUTION

Colobine monkeys range from Sechuan in China, and Southeast Asia, Indonesia, and India west to Africa; they are also present on many oceanic islands. *Pygathrix* and *Nasalis* range from southern China, through Southeast Asia to the Mentawai Islands and Borneo, but are not found on the Malay Peninsula or Sumatra. Other Asian species range from a latitude of around 35°N at the Afghanistan/Pakistan border to Lombok in the Lesser Sunda Islands. African species occur from Senegal and the Gambia, through the forests of Guinea and central Africa to Ethiopia. There are a few remote populations in East Africa and on the islands of Fernando Po and Zanzibar.

FOOD AND FEEDING

The leaf monkeys earned their name with good reason, as there are a few colobine species that eat only leaves: These include the Tonkin snub-nosed monkey, the Mentawai Islands sureli, Barbe's leaf monkey, and the Guinea forest black colobus. All species except Brelich's snub-nose eat leaves to some degree: For example, the purple-faced langur's diet comprises 60 percent leaf matter, 28 percent fruits, and 12 percent blossoms. Moreover, just three tree species supply it with nearly three-quarters of its diet. Indeed, most colobine species eat miscellaneous tree or shrub parts—flowers, seeds, bulbs, and shoots—but to pigeonhole the entire subfamily as a group of tree- or shrub-browsers does little justice to their versatility.

WHAT'S ON THE MENU?

Colobines take what is offered in their particular habitats—within the broad confines of vegetation, mineral deposits, and insect life. For example, colobuses, leaf monkeys, and Hanuman langurs consume soil or the clay from termite mounds, while the golden leaf monkey eats salty earth and sand, and the grizzled sureli is reported to stir up and eat silt from salt springs; in all these cases, the monkeys are deliberately taking in extra minerals, just as we might take a daily vitamin pill.

There are even more diverse delicacies on the colobine menu—including locusts and beetles, lichen, fungi, pith, plant roots, and rotten wood. We have seen how the availability of food sources—and the ability to digest them—affects the distribution of monkeys, and the habitats of certain colobine species present them with a very narrow

---

THE HANUMAN LANGUR CAN EAT FRUITS THAT CONTAIN ENOUGH STRYCHNINE TO KILL OTHER MONKEYS STONE DEAD

---

menu. Brelich's snub-nosed monkey lives at altitudes up to 7,500 ft (2,300 m) in the evergreen subtropical forest of China's Fan-jin mountain range. Here, it seems to dine exclusively on wild cherries, pears, and cucumbers. By the same token, more wide-ranging colobines seem to have earned their go-anywhere versatility by dint of a very tough stomach. Generally, as far as colobines are concerned, those forests with the richest soil play host to trees with more palatable foliage, whereas nutrient-poor soils are linked with tree foliage containing more plant defense chemicals.

(in)SIGHT

TRAVELS THROUGH THE STOMACH

Colobines have large, multichambered stomachs that allow for the processing of large volumes of rough vegetation.

The upper stomach chambers are free from strong acids, and this enables special gut bacteria to break down the high cellulose content in, for example, leathery tropical leaves, and thereby release energy. But the bacteria have another vital function: They can unlock and neutralize the toxins found in many food plants eaten by colobines. The minerals obtained from salt licks and other deposits sustain these helpful bacteria.

Tough and toxic, the food passes slowly through the colobine gut. The neutralized, part-processed vegetation passes from the upper stomach to the highly acidic lower parts, where it is further broken down and the last nutrients are gleaned before the remainder is processed for defecation.

Illustration Kim Thompson

FAST FOOD

Colobus monkeys (above) *spend nearly all the time in trees where their favorite food is never far from reach. After feeding they sit quietly to allow time for their leafy meal to be digested.*

Most colobines spend the larger part of their day either feeding or digesting their meals. The guereza, for example, spends about a fifth of the day eating, and some three-fifths resting while its stomach slowly breaks down the ingested cellulose. Colobines are fairly relaxed feeders. When a troop reaches a favorable feeding tree, the members usually spread out: There is plenty for everyone in the forest's canopy, midstory foliage, or lower shrub layer. Any latecomer to the "restaurant" is careful to pick its way unobtrusively among its companions to an empty "seat." Here it may sit sometimes for hours on end, peacefully plucking and investigating shoots and leaves with its fine, dexterous fingers before stuffing them into its mouth.

Feeding tends to peak in the morning and late afternoon but, because in many species' diets the food is not especially nutritious, a colobine needs to "snack" frequently through the day. This tends to tie up its time and prevent it from involved social interaction with its fellows.

A young proboscis monkey lacks the tonguelike, pendulous nose of the adult male.

The colobine eating apparatus is distinguished not only by a multichambered stomach (see box) but also by a lack of cheek pouches. The cercopithecine monkeys do have these extra stowage areas, although they lack the special stomach. These monkeys need to range more widely to find their fruit-dominated diet, which is more sporadic in distribution; they are also more ground-based, and must therefore run the gauntlet of more predators. So they use cheek pouches in much the same way that ruminants, such as wild cattle and deer, use their multichambered bellies: They bulk up on food, then retreat to a safer place in which to chew and digest.

For the colobines, however, food is that much more plentiful within a given area, and they do not require special knowledge to find it. Therefore there is less pressure to find food and, accordingly, reduced competition between individuals when they do find it—none of the mealtime squabbles that are typical of guenons or mangabeys, for example. As tree-feeders, colobines do not have to feed out in the open, where big cats and other predators have the upper hand. So, in this more relaxed environment, there is no need for the cheek pouches. ■

SOCIAL STRUCTURE

A ll colobine monkeys are social to some degree. Family units or troops range from a single monogamous pair plus offspring—as in the case of the Mentawai Islands sureli—to the vast, 600-strong "herds" of golden monkeys that reportedly have been seen in the Chinese mountains. In most species, a typical troop contains up to 40 individuals. The satanic black and Pennant's red colobuses form troops up to 80 strong, while the proboscis monkey, red-shanked douc, and Guinea forest red colobus reach around the 60 mark. Much smaller troops are typical of the surelis, the hooded black, purple-faced, and capped leaf monkeys, the guereza (one of the black colobus species), and the pig-tailed snub-nosed monkey. In these species, troops usually number fewer than a dozen close relatives.

TROOP TYPES

Although colobine societies are less strictly structured than other monkeys, each species tends to associate in social units of a fixed nature. One of the most common of these is the single-male troop, where one adult male rules a harem of females plus their attendant young of various years; he dictates who gets to mate (usually him alone). This troop type occurs in almost all colobine species except the

KNOWN BY HIS NOSE

Proboscis monkey troops number up to thirty or so individuals and contain one or several males—the only members of the troop to have distinctive pendulous noses.

FLEXIBLE FAMILIES

Troop sizes among pig-tailed snub-noses vary depending on habitat disturbance: Where they are hunted, troops comprise a mated pair plus two or three offspring. In more remote areas a single male rules a harem of up to four females and their young.

1446

Robin Budden/Wildlife Art Agency

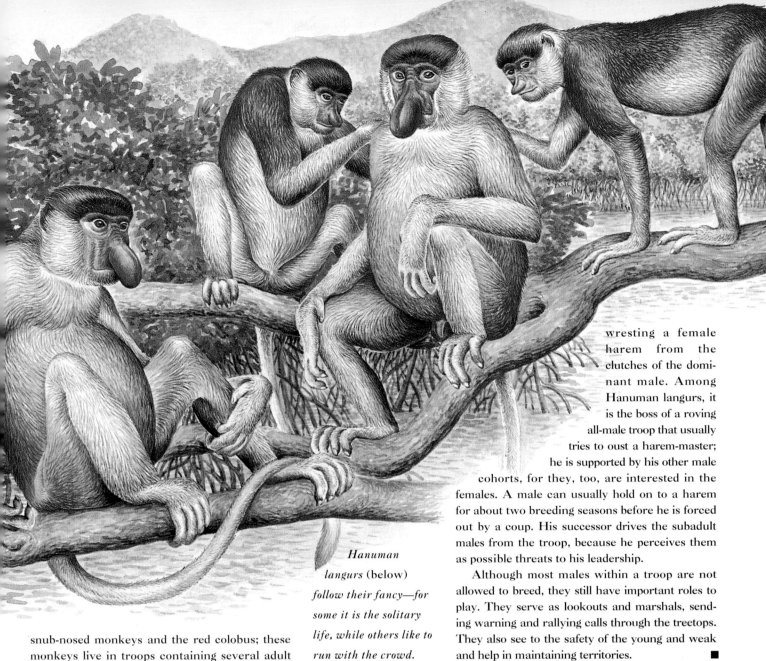

Hanuman langurs (below) *follow their fancy—for some it is the solitary life, while others like to run with the crowd.*

snub-nosed monkeys and the red colobus; these monkeys live in troops containing several adult males, with their own pecking order which includes a dominant individual. In any situation where a troop is male-dominated, that troop also holds a territory corresponding to its size.

To complicate matters, however, there are a number of species which display great flexibility in troop type. In the Hanuman langur, for example, troops may contain one or several ranked males. Still other Hanuman troops comprise a number of nonranked males; among these, the younger, less powerful males have to snatch at odd opportunities to breed, usually when the more dominating males let slip their guard for a brief moment. Their chances are good, for in any mixed troop there will be at least as many females as males, and usually there are plenty more. The fourth troop type is an all-male brotherhood; these gangs tend to be nomadic, and have their own social hierarchy. And there are also many species in which males live alone.

Although females tend to stay put for life in their family group, males live in continual hope of wresting a female harem from the clutches of the dominant male. Among Hanuman langurs, it is the boss of a roving all-male troop that usually tries to oust a harem-master; he is supported by his other male cohorts, for they, too, are interested in the females. A male can usually hold on to a harem for about two breeding seasons before he is forced out by a coup. His successor drives the subadult males from the troop, because he perceives them as possible threats to his leadership.

Although most males within a troop are not allowed to breed, they still have important roles to play. They serve as lookouts and marshals, sending warning and rallying calls through the treetops. They also see to the safety of the young and weak and help in maintaining territories. ■

TERRITORY

Given that most colobines live in habitats where food and shelter are not hard to come by, they can happily spend their lives within a limited stretch of forest—or, in the case of some species, open ground. This area is referred to as their home range. Such areas range greatly in size between species and also between different troops of a species, depending of course on the nature of the habitat—the terrain and availability of food trees.

More placid than other monkeys, colobines tend to be relaxed about the boundaries of their full home range. In several species, however, a troop may defend a core area of the range described as the territory: This "keep" will contain important feeding and resting trees. Such behavior is known in some surelis, leaf monkeys, langurs, and colobuses, and is displayed usually by the males, in the form of energetic calling and jumping about in the branches.

At daybreak, Mentawai langurs and banded leaf monkeys call out loudly and leap frenetically, to establish their troop's patch before feeding begins; these claims are reinforced daily. Purple-faced monkeys, living at high densities in a fairly small home range of 2.5–24.7 acres (1–10 hectares), are especially indignant to find trespassers on their territory, chasing them off with loud screams. They even rebuke members of their own troop that have been caught straying beyond the boundaries of home. Other species are less tenacious: The guereza will give chase to a trespasser, but may pretend not to notice it on another day. Pennant's red

Colobuses (right) *are famed for their territorial whoops, uttered at key points during the day.*

colobus territories may overlap greatly, although each troop is unlikely to kick up a fuss unless it unexpectedly bumps into other cohabitants. Should troops from farther afield stray in, however, they are not tolerated one bit.

Some of the most methodical and dramatic of territorial displays are seen in the pied colobuses, males in particular. Regular as clockwork, these monkeys perch on

RAIDING PARTY
A Hanuman langur troop will do its best not only to defend its own territory, but also to usurp that of a neighboring troop— and if necessary will fight hard to do so.

(in)SIGHT

HANUMAN KILLERS

An adult male Hanuman langur is notoriously aggressive when it comes to territoriality and troop takeovers. When he gains control of a harem, a male not only throws out other possible contenders but may also kill the resident infants. But this is not done out of sheer vindictiveness: As his instinctual motive is to mate and produce plenty of his own offspring, he needs sexually receptive females, and his days as leader are numbered from the start.

Female Hanumans gestate for about 28 weeks and produce babies roughly every 15–24 months. The male simply cannot afford to wait until the infants of his predecessor are weaned, so he kills them. Within a couple of weeks, each bereaved female will be sexually receptive. Of course, the females try to defend their own and other infants, often by carrying them to the thinnest branches, out of reach of the heavy male. They may well succeed in their efforts; a few infants undoubtedly survive this perilous period.

William Paten/Planet Earth Pictures

their sleeping tree and herald the dawn with deep, hoarse croaks that carry for miles through the forest. Soon, unseen neighboring troops answer the call.

Later, when the colobus troop reaches its morning feeding site, the males renew their calling, particularly if they detect other troops nearby. They climb up into the canopy and jump excitedly about, leaping among the branches and shaking them vigorously, while also showing off their bold black and white coat markings. The other troops in the area respond with equal exuberance as soon as the first troop has finished, after which they all settle down for a feed.

By making its location clear to its neighbors, a troop minimizes the risk of being startled by chance encounters in the forest, which could spark hostilities. ∎

LIFE CYCLE

Among colobine species living in seasonal climates, births tend to peak in certain seasons. The peaks are usually, but not always, timed to coincide with the maximum food availability.

THE MATING GAME

Where there is a defined breeding season, lone males and bachelor groups start to increase the pressure on stable harem herds, hoping for a chance to mate; tempers at this time can flare up into fights.

Interestingly, in many colobines, the female initiates mating. The female pied colobus, for example, has more-or-less permanent genital swellings, whereas in many other monkeys the genital area swells only when she is sexually receptive. So in order to catch the male's attention, she first casts a suggestive glance at him: lips pursed, mouth closed. If he ignores her pouting, she may well smack or bite him, or eventually thrust her rump in his face. Her gesture is finally clear to him, and he decides upon a suitable site for their coupling.

Gestation periods range from 140–210 days depending on the species. The female leaves the troop early in the morning to give birth to a single infant (twins are rare)—partly to avoid predators, but also to allow plenty of time for suckling. She is

FEMALE FLIRTS
Among many colobuses the female makes the first move in mating; She pouts provocatively at the male to attract his attention.

BABY-SITTERS
Females fulfill a useful role as wet nurses to the infants of other mothers, and can often be seen suckling an infant at each nipple.

(in)SIGHT

FAKING IT

Life can be hard for a female Hanuman langur. Having invested around 30 weeks' gestation—and plenty of care and attention— upon her infant, it must come as a bitter blow when a new male deposes her former mate and wrests control of the harem. For he will deliberately—and repeatedly, if necessary—try to kill her offspring and bring her back into breeding condition so that she can bear his infant.

However, the female can avoid this situation by putting into effect a scheme of her own. Her aim is to satisfy her new master's reproductive urges, and she can do this through effecting a "phantom estrus"; simply by pretending to be sexually receptive she attracts the male, who mates with her and, wrongly confident that he has sown his own genes, may well spare her infant.

soon back with the troop, however, to show off the infant that clings nervously to her belly; it is then enthusiastically handled and passed around by all her female relatives. This "show and tell" is undertaken by all colobines except the red colobus and pale-thighed sureli. The male pied colobuses show little enthusiasm for their new troop member, although the infant's father may become protective toward it.

The infant's coat color is a distinctive feature of these monkeys: In all langurs and leaf monkeys except the Hanuman, the newborn is a bright yellow or orange. The infant pied colobus is brilliant white, gaining adult coloration after two to four months. Well developed at birth, it starts to nibble on leaves after only five weeks, although it may

GROWING UP

The life of an olive colobus

A MOUTHFUL

The olive colobus is unique among monkeys in carrying her offspring in her mouth for the first few weeks of its life.

are suckled or fawned over by all their sisters, cousins, and aunts, but rough or inexperienced treatment from any of these prompts the mother to grab her offspring back again. Leaving her infant alone or with another female does, at least, give a mother time to catch up on feeding; it also helps to toughen up the youngster for the difficult months ahead.

Upon reaching independence, a young male will usually leave the natal troop and join an all-male gang. Young females stay with their elder relatives, joining in grooming sessions and taking an interest in the other infants. ■

Like most colobines, these female colobus or guereza monkeys enjoy playing the role of "auntie."

Larry Tacker/Planet Earth Pictures

continue to suckle from its mother or other related females for up to fifteen months. Usually, however, its confidence and independence grow to the extent that, at four months old, the youngster is feeding and exploring its environment, hitching only the occasional ride on its mother's belly when the troop moves on. The young colobus reaches adult size at two years of age.

As in the colobus, newborn Hanuman langurs

FAMILY TIES

The infant gets about by clinging to its mother's belly, and remains close by her until, after several weeks, it has mustered the confidence to explore its surroundings alone.

FROM BIRTH TO DEATH

HANUMAN LANGUR
GESTATION: 190–210 DAYS
NO OF YOUNG: 1, TWINS OCCASIONALLY IN HIMALAYAN POPULATIONS
BREEDING: AT ANY TIME, BUT PEAKS IN LOCAL DRY SEASON
WEIGHT AT BIRTH: 14 OZ (400 G)
EYES OPEN: AT BIRTH
WEANING: 10–12 MONTHS
SEXUAL MATURITY: FEMALE 2–4 YEARS, MALE 4 YEARS
LONGEVITY: 25 YEARS IN CAPTIVITY

SOUTHERN PIED COLOBUS
GESTATION: ABOUT 147–178 DAYS
NO OF YOUNG: 1
BREEDING: ANY TIME OF YEAR
WEIGHT AT BIRTH: 16 OZ (450 G)
EYES OPEN: AT BIRTH
WEANING: 15 MONTHS
SEXUAL MATURITY: FEMALE 2 YEARS, MALE 4 YEARS
LONGEVITY: 23 YEARS OR MORE IN CAPTIVITY

Illustrations Carol Roberts

POOR RELATIONS

WHEN IT COMES TO MONKEYS, WE HUMANS TEND TO DEAL IN DOUBLE STANDARDS. WE LOVE TO SEE THEM FOOL ABOUT IN THE ZOO, BUT GIVE THEM LITTLE PRECIOUS QUALITY OF LIFE IN THEIR NATURAL HABITATS

The hot, dusty roads of Jodhpur, India, are a riot of color: Market traders are setting up their stalls of vegetables, fruit, meat, and flowers, and bright textiles are draped over a stand. One stall holder is doing a roaring trade selling bananas—but as soon as he passes a ripe bunch to a tourist, a lithe, gray-brown monkey scampers up and, with lightning speed, pinches the fruit from the bewildered customer and hops up to the safety of a low rooftop, where it peels the fruit and crams it into its mouth. Down the road, another young primate has deftly stolen a soft drink carton from a child and casually sucks the sweet liquid through a plastic straw: The Hanuman monkeys are in town.

These acts of highway robbery are a daily fact of life in India, where the Hanuman is revered for its religious significance. Indeed, on Tuesdays—Hanuman Day—the locals actively feed the monkeys on choice tidbits. The monkey is tolerated to such an extent that, in some areas, troops derive as much as 90 percent of their diet from human settlements. Unfortunately, they do not stop at handouts: They also raid crops, taking so much food that farmers may lose a significant proportion of their harvest. On one notable occasion, exasperated villagers rounded up a Hanuman troop, loaded them onto a train, and dispatched them to the next district!

THE RELATIONSHIP SOURS

We may smile at these antics and praise these people for the affection they lavish upon this species, but this "relationship" is in danger of turning sour. Holy monkey or not, the Hanuman can put an unbearable strain on food supplies in districts where soaring human populations are themselves no strangers to hunger and poverty. Moreover, it is rapidly losing its more natural habitat—the forest—as farmland and settlements continue to encroach upon it.

Existing within this uneasy equilibrium with mankind, the Hanuman is probably one of the luckier colobines. Elsewhere, Old World monkeys are generally viewed by native peoples either as a good source of protein or, simply, as the occupiers of land that is ripe for development. Their range, which in the mainland features the world's warmer forested regions, coincides with those developing countries most in need of life's basic necessities, such as food, farmland, and fuelwood. Many inhabitants of developing nations do not have access to

Like many colobus species, the guereza (above) *has been hunted for its luxuriant, patterned mantle.*

Tom McHugh/Oxford Scientific Films

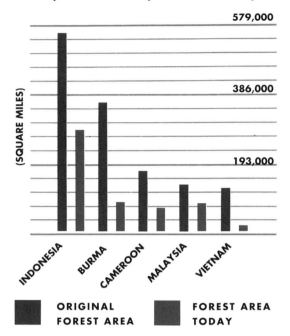

THEN & NOW

This graph shows the extent of deforestation and subsequent habitat loss of the colobine monkeys

579,000

386,000

(SQUARE MILES)

193,000

INDONESIA   BURMA   CAMEROON   MALAYSIA   VIETNAM

■ ORIGINAL FOREST AREA   ■ FOREST AREA TODAY

LOSS OF HABITAT

Among those countries that contain colobine species, Indonesia stands out among the rest in terms of habitat loss. But this is due chiefly to its sheer enormity, and the country still possesses about half the original area of wild habitat. Vietnam, by contrast, is a relatively small country—less than a quarter of the size of Indonesia— nestling in the Gulf of Tonkin in the South China Sea. It has lost a shocking four-fifths of its original forests, which host many rare colobine species.

efficient fossil fuels, such as oil and gas, to produce heat and light. These are largely imported and therefore expensive. Instead, they use timber. Forests regenerate too slowly for the rising populations, and by 1980 well over a billion people throughout the world were short of fuelwood. People in such dire straits cannot give priority to the monkeys of the forests.

PRECIOUS PELTS

Habitat loss through deforestation is a relatively modern threat, and colobine monkeys have long had to contend with much more besides. The lustrous

Doucs are among the many colobines threatened by deforestation and human conflict in Vietnam.

1453

black-and-white coat fringes, or mantles, of the pied and black colobus species have been sought after since ancient times as body adornments and status symbols. The guereza's mantle, for example, was worn by Masai and other African tribes, and in particular by the witch doctors of many villages. The explorer Marco Polo, who journeyed into central Asia in the 13th century, described how the Mongol Khans wore capes about their shoulders made from colobus pelts.

Conducted at such a level, the colobus fur trade might have remained sustainable, but demand rose to dizzying heights in the 19th century when the pelts became fashionable among the ladies of European high society. The skins have also been used for such diverse products as bicycle saddles, dance costumes, hats, and tourist trophies. The monkeys are still hunted today, but the demand for their fur has now diminished. In the mainland, the various species have survived the onslaught, although localized races in isolated forests have been wiped out to fuel the vagaries of fashion just as surely as deforestation has depleted their habitat.

In many parts of Africa and Asia, monkey parts are either eaten or listed among the ingredients of

> COLOBINE MONKEY PELTS ONCE
> FEATURED IN THE CEREMONIAL
> GARMENTS OF CHINESE NOBILITY

traditional medicines. The flesh of the Nilgiri langur is used in treatments for respiratory ailments, while that of the olive colobus is considered a delicacy. The doucs are eaten in Vietnam, and the pig-tailed snub-nosed leaf monkey is heavily hunted for food on the Mentawai Islands off the coast of Sumatra. These islands are also being logged for their valuable timber at a frightening rate, and this large species is known to survive only in primary (undisturbed) forest. On the Mentawai Islands and in many other forested parts of developing nations, it is the inroads created by logging companies that enable other interested parties access to the forests' treasures.

MANGROVE MADNESS

Deforestation of a special kind has begun to affect the proboscis and silvered leaf monkeys. They live in mangroves, which, by dint of their treacherous swamps and seasonal flooding, were out of man's grasp until comparatively recently. Indeed, the easiest way of studying these species even today is by boat rather than foot. But mangroves hold rich rewards for those who manage to exploit them, and in recent years the developed nations have

R. van Nostrand/Frank Lane Picture Agency

THE CHINA STORY

The golden snub-nose lives in vast troops of up to 600 in its Chinese mountain refuges. In Szechuan and Gansu, by the Red River Basin, this monkey inhabitats both evergreen and deciduous forests, where it frequents the rhododendron thickets and rarely comes down to the ground. Its alternative name of "snow monkey" testifies to the forbidding mountain climate.

The French missionary and biologist Père Armand David was the first Westerner to describe the golden monkey. After a visit to China in 1869, he took six specimens back to Paris, where colleagues from the Museum of Natural History were charmed by the monkey's tiny snub nose, blue facial skin, and golden mane. They named it *Rhinopithecus roxellana* in honor of Roxellana, a Galician slave girl who was abducted into the harem of a 16th-century sultan, Suleiman the Magnificent. Her tilted nose, big blue eyes, and flowing golden hair so captured the Turk's heart that he married her.

Roxellana's namesake held a powerful magic for the Chinese, too. For a thousand years at least, the lustrous orange-tinged mantle of the golden monkey was used to make coveted garments. Not only was it beautiful, it was also reputed to prevent rheumatism, and its flesh and bones were

CONSERVATION MEASURES

● Hunting of Biet's snub-nosed monkey has been banned in China since 1975.

● The golden snub-nosed monkey is protected inasmuch as its range includes the Wolong Nature Reserve. This 772-sq-mile (2,000-sq-km) area of mainly bamboo forest in the Qionglai Mountains is a vital stronghold of the giant panda—a species whose protection has full government support.

ught after for medicinal remedies.

Luckily the wearing of the mantle was served only for the nobility of the anchu dynasty. Nevertheless, this mon-ey bore a high price on its head and was unted down, to the extent that only some 700–5,700 survive today. Today it is an fense, punishable by fines or even prisonment, to capture or kill the golden onkey, but even as late as 1985 it was ported that local communities were agaged in mass roundups of the species.

China's other two snub-nosed monkeys e even rarer. There are probably only 00 Brelich's snub-noses left in Guizhou, hile Biet's snub-nose is critically endan-ered, with only 200 or so individuals.

Kenneth W. Fink/Ardea

BEAUTIFUL BUT BELEAGUERED—THE GOLDEN SNUB-NOSED MONKEY OF CHINA.

The following colobine species re listed in Appendix 1 of CITES, the Convention on nternational Trade in Endangered Species, which orbids international trade in he species or its body parts vithout special permit: Mentawai and Hanuman angurs, golden and capped eaf monkeys, doucs, and the big-tailed snub-nosed nonkey.

COLOBINES IN DANGER

PIG-TAILED SNUB-NOSED MONKEY	ENDANGERED
GRIZZLED LEAF MONKEY	ENDANGERED
MENTAWAI LANGUR	ENDANGERED
TONKIN SNUB-NOSED MONKEY	ENDANGERED
BRELICH'S SNUB-NOSED MONKEY	ENDANGERED
RED-SHANKED DOUC	ENDANGERED
FRANÇOIS' LEAF MONKEY	ENDANGERED
WESTERN PIED COLOBUS	VULNERABLE
SATANIC BLACK COLOBUS	VULNERABLE
GEOFFROY'S PIED COLOBUS	VULNERABLE
PROBOSCIS MONKEY	VULNERABLE
OLIVE COLOBUS	VULNERABLE
GOLDEN SNUB-NOSED MONKEY	VULNERABLE
GOLDEN LANGUR	RARE
NILGIRI LANGUR	INSUFFICIENTLY KNOWN

ENDANGERED MEANS THAT THE SURVIVAL OF THE ANIMAL IS UNLIKELY UNLESS STEPS ARE TAKEN TO SAVE IT. VULNERABLE MEANS THAT THE ANIMAL IS LIKELY TO MOVE INTO THE ENDANGERED CATEGORY IF THINGS CONTINUE AS THEY ARE. RARE INDICATES THAT THE ANIMAL RISKS BECOMING ENDANGERED OR VULNERABLE. INSUFFICIENTLY KNOWN MEANS THAT THE ANIMAL IS SUSPECTED TO BELONG TO ONE OF THE ABOVE CATEGORIES, BUT THERE IS TOO LITTLE INFORMATION TO BE SURE.

been able to clear-cut mangroves due to improved agricultural technology.

They have also led the way in converting coastal swamps to fish farms and other farming practices. Mangrove timber is cut for fuelwood, building timber, and charcoal, and the high tannin content in the bark of mangroves makes it useful in leather production. Rice paddies, too, account for much of the mangrove destruction.

Any commercial activity in these coastal swamp forests is bound to upset their fragile ecological bal-ance; quite apart from stripping the monkeys of a home, they also cause dire problems for the local human population. Mangroves play a vital role in taking the brunt of sea storms; when the man-groves are cleared, the low coastal plains can easily flood, leading to widespread famine.

Also at risk are peat swamp forests, which are widespread across Borneo and are an important habitat for the proboscis monkey. Peat swamps act as vast natural sponges, storing freshwater, and support important forests. Peat is being cut for hor-ticulture and other industries, and there is pressure on Malaysia to burn peat rather than fuelwood and imported fossil fuels.

POPULATION PRESSURE

In addition to felling its forests for their precious timber, Indonesia has usurped land for the purposes of human resettlement. Among the 13,670 islands that comprise the Indonesian archipelago, many are cloaked in lush forests and have been havens for wildlife for centuries. The majority of the country's population is crammed onto the islands of Java, Bali, and Madura, and the Indonesian government recently started to move many of its people to more remote areas, including the forests of Kalimantan in Borneo and West Irian, New Guinea. Borneo is a key stronghold for colobine species, and the habitat disturbance or outright clearance resulting from the mass influx of settlers can only spell trouble for the monkeys in the long term.

More deliberate destruction has been wreaked in Sarawak, Malaysian territory lying in the north of Borneo. Here, timber production was tripled between 1977an 1990, and Sarawak has already lost more than a quarter, in area, of its original forests. It is estimated that, at such a high rate of deforestation, most if not all of Sarawak's primary forest will have fallen by the year 2000. Due to population pressure and a demand for more resources, the cleared land is being farmed to the point where nutrients are exhausted and the soil is eroded. Malaysia has been forced to strip the natural resources of Sarawak—and neighboring Sabah—

ALONGSIDE MAN

A LIVING LEGEND

Perhaps because of their close resemblance to man, monkeys hold a special place in human culture, and few monkeys are held in higher esteem than the Hanuman langur.

The Hanuman features in a famous epic, the *Ramayana*, which was written in India over 2,000 years ago. The story tells of how Sita, the wife of the god Rama, is carried off by the demon king Ravana to his stronghold in the city of Lanka. Rama enlists the help of the monkey king Sugriva and his general, Hanuman. Hanuman marches at the head of his monkey troops and lays seige to Lanka, setting fire to it. In the process of rescuing Sita, Hanuman suffers burns to his face and hands; according to legend, this is why the monkey today has a black face and paws.

The *Ramayana* is an often-told legend in India, and every Tuesday in towns and villages throughout the country, people feed the monkeys—along with peacocks and other venerated animals. The tameness consequently shown by many Hanuman troops has enabled scientists in India to study them closely and gain valuable insights into their behavior.

Hans Reinhard/Bruce Coleman Ltd.

as it is not permitted to export timber from the main peninsula. The demand for timber is higher than ever, however, especially from Japan, Taiwan, and Korea, and Malaysia simply cannot afford to preserve its rich natural resources rather than make a short-term profit—and so the monkeys have to go.

Away to the north of Malaysia, Vietnam has suffered immeasurable losses, among both its people and its wildlife. Together with limited areas of tropical rain forest, its bamboo, monsoon, and

The sacred Hanuman langur commands great respect in India, and it exploits this favor to the full.

swamp forests are home to the Tonkin snub-nosed monkeys and doucs, and the ebony, François', and silvered leaf monkeys. Most, if not all, of these species are hunted for food, and the doucs in particular have been hard hit—and not only in recent times. On one occasion in 1819 the crew of a ship docked at Da Nang disembarked into the local forests and shot more than 100 doucs in a single morning. It appeared that the monkeys, which normally faced little intrusion from local people, had yet to discover that firearms were lethal. After repeated attacks, however, they soon learned to melt into the canopy at the first crack of a rifle.

Isolated incidents such as these, however, pale into insignificance when set against the wholesale devastation that resulted from nearly thirty years of war on Vietnamese soil. The conflict which had been raging since 1946 suddenly escalated in 1965, when the United States stepped in. The high explosive bombs, napalm, and leaf-stripping chemicals dropped from U.S. planes resulted in human casualties on an horrific scale, but also laid waste to vast swaths of forest.

It is impossible to calculate their effects upon the wildlife of the region, but in that same Da Nang region where seamen slew so many doucs, observers counted only thity to forty of these monkeys in the space of ten weeks in 1974. Today, northern Vietnam remains a critically dangerous place for Old World monkeys, since forest clearance and agriculture are still permitted and there are insufficient wildlife preserves in the region. ■

INTO THE FUTURE

Deforestation is probably the single greatest threat to colobine monkeys; sadly, there is little evidence that those countries rich in forest species are going to stop destroying their natural resources. Malaysia has simply diverted its logging activities from the mainland to Borneo, and slash-and-burn clearance is a pressing problem in Africa, northern Vietnam, and many other countries. Even the less extreme practice of selective, sustainable logging does little to preserve colobines, since many species are dependent upon primary (undisturbed) forest.

Ironically, one area in which colobines are "lucky" is that of scientific research, which involves the live experimentation upon animals for medicinal, cosmetic, and academic purposes. Figures for 1991 show that, in the British field of primate research, more than 50 percent of experiments were conducted upon New World primates, such as marmosets

PREDICTION

GOOD NEWS FOR PRIMATES

In 1994, Indonesia banned the live export of its primates; while this does not directly affect colobines, it is nevertheless extremely encouraging and will hopefully produce a side effect not only in general primate protection but habitat preservation also.

and tamarins; the rest involved mainly Old World monkeys such as macaques and baboons, while colobines barely featured in the statistics. This is probably because colobine monkeys are among the most difficult primates to keep in captivity, especially under laboratory conditions. Their leafy diets are often hard to duplicate or substitute, while many other primates, like rhesus monkeys, are opportunistic feeders and easier to care for.

A few countries in Southeast Asia have started to try to reverse the destruction of their mangroves. In Indonesia, Thailand, and Malaysia, a certain amount of mangrove exploitation has for many years been managed sustainably through "crop rotation" and the replanting of seedlings. However, this careful management has so far applied mainly for its commercial benefits rather than in the interests of wildlife, and the areas concerned are unlikely to continue to support viable monkey populations. ■

RAMSAR CONVENTION

The Convention on Wetlands of International Importance Especially as Wetland Habitat is generally better known as the Ramsar Convention, named after the town in Iran where it was created in 1971. The convention is a special forum for promoting conservation of the world's wetlands, with additional legal powers of enforcement. By 1992, more than sixty countries worldwide had committed their intent to preserve a total of 546 sites by signing Ramsar's List of Wetlands of International Importance. These sites include mangroves and other coastal swamp forests, where the proboscis and silvered leaf monkey live—along with unique fish, birds, crabs, and other species. Signatories to the list are obliged to safeguard their wetland sites and insure that any commercial exploitation is managed at a sustainable level.

Clearly, however, many developing nations are under immense pressure to reap the short-term economic benefits of habitat clearance and development to meet the needs of their people. To counter this, Ramsar has established a fund, which gives financial support to those countries in need of capital to protect their wetlands.

CAPTIVE BREEDING

Captive breeding in zoos has met with some success in certain species, such as the Hanuman and dusky langurs, the proboscis monkey, the doucs, and the guereza. However, the potential for reintroduction of captive-bred stock to areas of former habitat depends on habitat protection. The future for colobine monkeys must lie in protected reserves within their natural habitat.

Illustration Simon Turvey/Wildlife Art Agency

MANDRILLS & OTHER OLD WORLD MONKEYS

RELATIONS

Old World monkeys belong
the primate order. Oth
members of this order includ

HUMAN

ORANGUTANS

GORILLAS

GIBBONS

CHIMPANZEES

NEW WORLD MONKEY

PROSIMIANS

Mitch Reardon/Tony Stone Worldwide

DAZZLING DIVERSITY

ADAPTABLE AND INTELLIGENT, THE OLD WORLD MONKEYS HAVE
EXPLOITED ALMOST EVERY TYPE OF HABITAT OPEN TO THEM,
DIVERSIFYING INTO A BEWILDERING VARIETY OF SPECIES

CLASSIFICATION

The Old World monkeys are usually considered the "typical" monkeys of Africa and southern Asia, a closely related group of primates that has diversified into the powerful baboons and drills, the adaptable macaques, the forest-dwelling mangabeys, and the agile, long-tailed guenons.

ORDER
Primates

SUBORDER
Anthropoidea
(higher primates)

FAMILY
Cercopithecidae
(Old World monkeys)

SUBFAMILY
Cercopithecinae
(guenons, macaques, and baboons)

GENERA
nineteen

SPECIES
ninety-four

Monkeys evolved around 35 million years ago in what is now Africa. The New World monkeys are believed to have crossed the oceans on floating vegetation to arrive on what was then the island continent of South America. Those that survived found themselves in a land without any other primates, while those remaining in Africa evolved into the family now known as the Cercopithecidae (serk-o-pith-ECK-id-ie). Eventually they spread into Asia too, and the Cercopithecidae are therefore known as the Old World monkeys.

Separated for so many years, Old and New World monkeys have evolved certain essential differences. The most obvious is the shape of their nostrils: wide open, far apart, and facing outward in species from the Americas; narrow, close together, and pointing downward in the Old World monkeys. Many of the New World monkeys also have muscular, prehensile tails, but none of the Old World

Unlike many of their smaller relatives, the baboons are adapted for life on the ground.

species do. Why they lack such a useful appendage is a mystery.

Like all monkeys, the Old World species are typically inquisitive and skilled with their hands, having acquired considerable intelligence and a degree of manual dexterity almost unparalleled in the animal kingdom. Many species have strong opposable thumbs that enable them to pick and sort through food with great precision. Some, notably most of the small, agile guenons, live primarily in the trees; others, such as the baboons and many of the macaques, spend their lives on the ground.

There are ninety-four species in all, encompassing an extraordinary variety of sizes, shapes, lifestyles, and diets. Sizes range from the 4-oz (120-g) talapoin—the size of a squirrel—to the 110-lb (50-kg) mandrill—the size of a St. Bernard dog. They have conquered every habitat from seashores and mangrove swamps to hot dry savannas, steamy tropical jungles, and snow-strewn slopes of high mountains. While some species eat only fruit and

Adrian Warren/Ardea

Carlo Dani & Ingrid Jeske/Natural Science Pictures

The spectacular facial colors of the male mandrill (above) make him a particularly striking primate.

1460

Adaptable species such as the vervet (below) have become widespread and common over vast areas.

Nick Gordon/Ardea

leaves, others are generalists. Some eat meat and may even hunt and kill it. Their social organization is also varied, with some species living in small family groups, some in troops run by older females, and some in large male-dominated bands.

The areas inhabited by various species also differ widely. Species such as the olive baboon and the vervet monkey are to be found over vast areas—almost half a continent in the case of the vervet—while others, such as the Celebes macaque, are confined to small islands.

Tracing the evolution of this diverse group of animals is not easy, owing to a shortage of suitably preserved fossils, but it seems clear that the Pleistocene Ice Age, which gripped the planet some 16,000–12,000 years ago, played a major part in the

(in)SIGHT

MONKEY MISFITS

All guenons are in the same family and most belong to the same genus, but some species are sufficiently different to be placed in other genera. Among these are the patas monkey, talapoin, and Allen's swamp monkey. Patas monkeys live in dry, open country in Ethiopia, Kenya, and Tanzania and, unusually, live mainly on the ground. Allen's swamp monkey is another ground-dweller that has evolved to resemble a baboon, while the talapoin, the smallest of the guenons, has a number of unusual communication habits.

story. During this period the earth's climate became much drier as much of its moisture became locked up in ice, and as a result sea levels fell, grasslands expanded, and forest cover contracted.

The differences this made to the Old World monkeys were profound. In continental Africa and mainland Asia, some populations of forest species died as their habitat disappeared. Others, fortunate enough to be living in areas of high rainfall, survived. Living in isolation, these small populations probably had no contact with each other, and slowly the isolated primates began to accumulate random differences in body color, call type, and behavior.

But primates are nothing if not adaptable, and the expansion of the grasslands provided other populations with the opportunity to colonize a new habitat, adapting their behavior, social organization, color patterns, and anatomy to suit. In this way sister species arose—one adapted to the grasslands, one to the forests. This can be seen today in the vervet monkey and the diana monkey. Similar events have occurred at least eight times since primates evolved, and this pattern of forest and grassland sister species is quite common. It explains the evolution of baboons (grassland) and drills and mandrills (forest)—indeed, many scientists believe that humans arose as the grassland sister species to the forest-living ancestors of the chimpanzee. ■

THE OLD WORLD MONKEYS' FAMILY TREE

The Old World monkey family Cercopithecidae is divided into two subfamilies: the Colobinae (coll-o-BEEN-ie) or leaf monkeys, and the Cercopithecinae (serk-o-pith-ECK-in-ie). The latter consists of four main groups: the macaques, the guenons, the mangabeys, and the baboons. Although closely related, the various types have evolved in very different ways and colonized a variety of habitats.

RHESUS MACAQUE

Macaca mulatta

(*mack-ACK-ah moo-LAT-ah*)

The adaptable rhesus macaque is typical of this opportunist group of monkeys. A familiar denizen of towns in northern India, it has been widely used in psychological and medical research and has given its name to the rhesus factor also found in human blood.

OTHER SPECIES:
14 INCLUDING
MOOR MACAQUE
BARBARY MACAQUE
BONNET MACAQUE

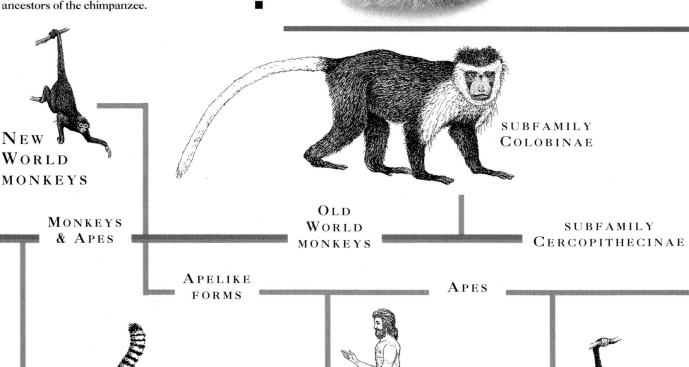

PRIMATES

NEW WORLD MONKEYS

MONKEYS & APES

SUBFAMILY COLOBINAE

OLD WORLD MONKEYS

SUBFAMILY CERCOPITHECINAE

APELIKE FORMS

APES

PROSIMIANS

HUMANS

GIBBONS

VERVET
Cercopithecus aethiops
(ser-co-pith-ECK-us IE-thee-ops)

The most widespread of the guenons, the vervet, grivet, or green monkey lives both on the ground and in the trees, foraging in large troops for a wide range of foods including fruit, flowers, leaves, and birds' eggs. It has the typical long tail and agile, lightweight build of this mainly forest-living group of monkeys, several of which spend most of their lives in the canopy high above the forest floor.

OTHER SPECIES:
19 INCLUDING
BLUE GUENON
MONA MONKEY
OWL-FACED
 MONKEY
DE BRAZZA'S
 MONKEY
REDTAIL MONKEY
PATAS MONKEY

WHITE MANGABEY
Cercocebus torquatus
(ser-co-SEE-bus tork-AHT-us)

The white mangabey is restricted to the primary rain forests of West Africa, where it forages on the ground for nuts, fruit, and leaves. Closely related to the baboons, the mangabeys are a small group of long-tailed forest monkeys with strong incisor teeth that enable them to crack the shells of nuts that are too hard for other monkeys.

OTHER SPECIES
BLACK MANGABEY
GRAY-CHEEKED
 MANGABEY
AGILE MANGABEY

Color illustrations Steve Kingston

MANDRILL
Mandrillus sphinx
(man-DRILL-us sfinks)

The spectacular male mandrill is the largest of the Old World monkeys. Like its relative the drill, it feeds on the forest floor in the tropical rain forests of western central Africa. The drills are essentially the forest equivalents of the mainly ground-dwelling baboons that live in open woods and savannas, often in large troops.

OTHER SPECIES:
DRILL
SAVANNA BABOON
GUINEA BABOON
GELADA
HAMADRYAS BABOON

B/W illustrations Ruth Grewcock & Peter David Scott

GREAT APES

ANATOMY: THE MANDRILL

The adult male mandrill is the biggest of the Old World monkeys, growing to a head-and-body length of some 31 in (80 cm). The smallest species is the talapoin monkey, one of the guenons, which grows to a head-and-body length of about 14 in (35 cm).

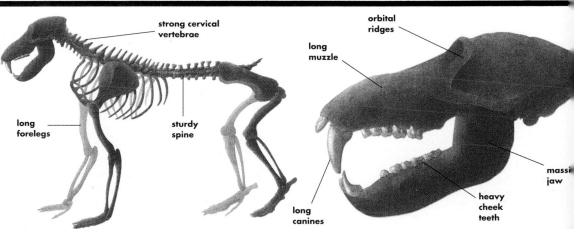

THE EYES

Monkeys are the only noncarnivorous mammals with forward-pointing eyes, giving binocular vision. Developed for judging distance in trees, this is also very useful for coordinating delicate actions during feeding and grooming.

LONG MUZZLE

A longer muzzle permits larger teeth, enhancing chewing power. The bulges are outgrowths of the nose bone. Set in a permanent snarl, the bright skin advertises the mandrill's maleness to rivals.

BEARD, CREST, AND MANE

Best developed in adult males, the crest and mane serve as a signal of status within the group. When bristled up they also display states of excitement, limiting potentially damaging aggression when conflicts occur between males.

THE HANDS

have long fingers and well-developed thumbs; these enable the mandrill to sort and process edible material with great precision, allowing it to exploit a wide range of food sources.

THE FORELEGS

are adapted for life on the ground, being longer than those of tree-dwelling monkeys to support the front of the body.

MACAQUE   **BABOON**   **GUENON**

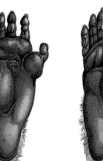

HANDS AND FEET

The hands (upper row) and the feet (lower row) are very similar, with long digits for grasping branches, but macaques have stronger thumbs than guenons, and baboons are more suited to standing on the ground.

MANDRILL SKELETON

The mandrill is adapted for life on all fours, with relatively long forelegs that support the body in a "head-up" stance. The heavy skull is supported by strong cervical vertebrae with long dorsal spines to anchor powerful neck muscles, and the rest of the spine is equally sturdy. The tailbones are fused and reduced to a stump.

strong cervical vertebrae

long forelegs

sturdy spine

orbital ridges

long muzzle

massive jaw

heavy cheek teeth

long canines

G-TAILED MACAQUE FACE POUT

BARBARY MACAQUE LIP SMACKING

RHESUS MACAQUE AGGRESSIVE STARE

FACIAL EXPRESSIONS

The faces of monkeys are highly expressive, although the meaning of each expression varies. An aggressive stare is clear, but a pouting face can precede an attack or an attempt to mate. Lip smacking in a male barbary macaque—but not in other species—signifies interest in an infant.

SHORT TAIL

Spending most of its life on the ground, the mandrill does not need a long tail for balance. A long tail could also obscure the display of the colorful buttocks.

COLORFUL BUTTOCKS

Mandrills live in deep, dense, dark rain forest. The colorful backside is thought to act as a flag, helping to keep the group together when moving through thick, dark vegetation. The colors penetrate particularly well through low light.

HEAVYSET BODY

The powerful, thickset body of the mandrill gives strength for defense against predators, for moving long distances in search of food, and for digging and overturning rocks while foraging.

FACT FILE:

THE MANDRILL

CLASSIFICATION

GENUS: *MANDRILLUS*

SPECIES: *SPHINX*

SIZE

HEAD–BODY LENGTH: UP TO 31 IN (80 CM)

TAIL LENGTH: 3 IN (7 CM)

HEIGHT AT SHOULDER: 20 IN (50 CM)

WEIGHT/MALE: UP TO 110 LB (50 KG)

WEIGHT/FEMALE: 60 LB (27 KG)

WEIGHT AT BIRTH: 18 OZ (500 G)

COLORATION

TAWNY GREEN FUR WITH YELLOWISH UNDERPARTS

MATURE MALE HAS BLUE CHEEKS SEPARATED BY A SCARLET NASAL RIDGE, FEMALE HAS BLACK FACE

LILAC BUTTOCK SKIN, TINGED RED AT THE EDGES

FEATURES

DRAMATIC, COLORFUL FACE IN MALE

FORWARD-FACING, CLOSE-SET EYES

LONG MUZZLE

BRIGHT BUTTOCK SKIN

POWERFUL BUILD

LONG ARMS

THE FEET

have long toes for gripping branches, although the mandrill spends most of its time on the ground, but the soles are longer than those of most monkeys.

SKULL AND TEETH

Like other baboons, the mandrill has a long muzzle accommodating an impressive array of teeth. The large canines of the male are mainly symbolic, for threatening other males, though they can be used to attack predators if required. The heavy cheek teeth provide chewing power, backed up by the massive jaw. The forward-facing eyes are protected by strong ridges of bone.

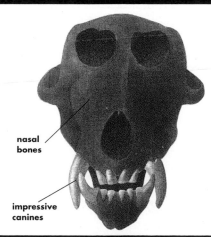

nasal bones

impressive canines

The expanded nasal bones act as bases for a facial signaling device. The grooves, when covered in flesh, mimic the ridged muzzle of a snarling animal and give the male a permanent expression of aggression at minimal energy cost. When combined with the yawning display of the long canines, the effect is impressive, earning the mandrill an undeserved reputation for ferocity.

MANDRILL FACIAL MUSCLES

ALMOST HUMAN

THE OLD WORLD MONKEYS HAVE EXCHANGED PHYSICAL SPECIALIZATION FOR A HIGHLY DEVELOPED INTELLIGENCE THAT ALLOWS THEM TO TURN ALMOST ANY SITUATION TO THEIR OWN ADVANTAGE

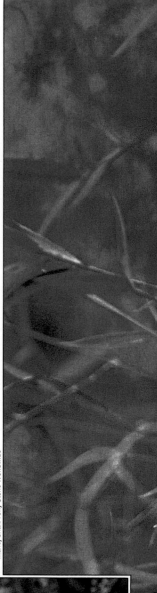

Manoj Shah/Tony Stone Worldwide

Long before the development of modern theories of evolution, and the idea that monkeys are intimately involved in our ancestry, people recognized something human about the way they behave. The notion is partly fanciful, like most human ideas about animals, but there is also a lot of truth in it. Monkeys do behave much like us, and for good reasons.

Unlike many mammals, the Old World monkeys have not evolved a battery of physical and instinctive adaptations to a particular way of life. Many species such as the macaques are relatively unspecialized, giving them the potential to exploit a huge variety of habitats and foods, and they are able to realize that potential because they have developed a tool that can be used in any situation: a refined, problem-solving intelligence.

WHEN A MONKEY USES ITS INTELLIGENCE TO SOLVE A PROBLEM, IT CAN DEMONSTRATE ITS SOLUTION TO OTHERS

Relying on intelligence brings problems early in life. A juvenile monkey cannot depend on its instincts to preserve it from danger and provide it with suitable food, since its instincts have been suppressed to allow a more opportunistic response to situations as they arise. So a young monkey must learn about the world by copying its mother and any other adults with which it lives. This can be a protracted business and makes early independence impossible. It also ties the mother to several years of childcare, but since the young develop into companions as well as heirs, the investment pays off.

The copying response is itself an instinct, of course, but it is infinitely more flexible than the type of rigid mental programming that makes the behavior of many other animals so predictable. This is because copying involves the transfer of information, and when one monkey acquires a new piece of information, it can pass this on, via the copying response, to others. So when an individual monkey uses its intelligence to solve a problem, it can demonstrate its solution to any other monkeys that are open to suggestion, and the idea will become part of the behavioral repertoire.

In one well-studied group of Japanese macaques, for example, an 18-month-old female was seen to wash sweet potatoes to remove sand before eating them. Ten years later the idea had spread throughout the troop and was being transferred to the next generation. Naturally such a trait will only spread through the originator's sphere of influence, and as a result monkey behavior is very variable. So one group may spend much of its time

David C. Fritts/Oxford Scientific Films

Young Japanese macaques mimic the mating act (above). *Play is a key part of monkey education.*

in SIGHT

COLOR CODES

In forests where several species of guenons occur together and may travel together for much of the day, an individual guenon might easily lose track of the rest of its troop, especially when danger strikes and the animals take off at high speed. To avoid this, these deep forest animals have developed big blocks of color on their faces, shoulders, flanks, and thighs. These act as flags, flashing their species identity to their traveling companions.

However, some of the blocks of color are not normally seen when traveling. A deliberate display of these color blocks conveys a more specific message: either threatening or pacifying a rival, or attracting a mate. The monkey adopts particular postures to show off the colors to full advantage, going through a ritual behavior sequence that often ends with the color patch being covered up—signaling "end of message."

foraging in the trees for fruit while another group of the same species devotes hours to searching for nuts on the forest floor. This can make the zoologist's job difficult, since generalizations about the behavior of a single species are only valid if they apply to every known wild population of that species. Zoologists increasingly use the term "culture" to describe groups of primates that share particular patterns of behavior, and although they are less complex, such primate cultures have a lot in common with those of humans.

The development of intelligence among the Old World monkeys has been linked to their highly social lifestyles, since social success favors perceptive individuals that can take advantage of the strengths and weaknesses of others. Since their social communication is mainly visual, involving a rich repertoire of facial expressions and gestures (unlike that of dogs, say, which communicate primarily by scent), monkeys are well equipped to learn by example and develop their own individual skills, social or otherwise. Since the same process can be seen in action in any kindergarten, it is not surprising that people recognized the link between monkeys and men long before Darwin put the idea on a scientific footing. ■

The intelligence of monkeys such as these bonnet macaques probably developed for social reasons.

HABITATS

Some Old World monkeys occupy a wide range of habitats while others have become adapted to particular environments. Rhesus macaques, for example, are found from North Africa across to China and out to Japan. Within this huge geographical range, some populations live under near-desert conditions while others live amid deep Himalayan snow. Himalayan rhesus macaques sleep in trees but spend much of their day foraging on the ground for roots, leaves, and small herbs. The pattern of their day is heavily influenced by the seasons. In early spring they eat the tips of young fir trees, while later they feast on berries. In summer they feed on mushrooms and insects such as cicadas, while autumn finds them rummaging in the pine needles for pinecones and the nutritious seeds they contain. Winter is a tough time, spent licking sap from pine needles and digging for underground tubers and roots.

The Himalayan rhesus macaques' social system reflects their tough life in a vigorously seasonal environment. Unlike lowland rhesus, which breed almost year-round, these mountain monkeys breed once a year. This restricts social unrest to a short annual period and reduces the energy expended in aggressive interactions. Such calorific miserliness is essential if the animals are to build up sufficient energy reserves to survive the harsh winter.

By contrast with rhesus macaques, gelada baboons are restricted to a single habitat: the high

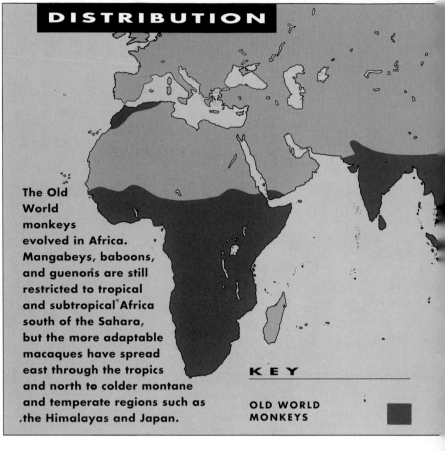

DISTRIBUTION

The Old World monkeys evolved in Africa. Mangabeys, baboons, and guenons are still restricted to tropical and subtropical Africa south of the Sahara, but the more adaptable macaques have spread east through the tropics and north to colder montane and temperate regions such as the Himalayas and Japan.

KEY

OLD WORLD MONKEYS

De Brazza's monkey, (below) *feeds both on the ground and in the trees in its tropical forest habitat.*

Tom McHugh/Oxford Scientific Films

FOCUS ON

GIBRALTAR

Gibraltar's "apes" are in fact barbary macaq possibly introduced from North Africa by the Romans. Limited habitat has weakened their social organization, resulting in more fights between individuals, but like other primates ir contact with humans, they have learned to exp the facilities their primate cousins have to offe They even drink from outside taps. However, may turn on any visitors who make "submissi responses to challenges, so the best defense is learn some monkey before visiting the Rock.

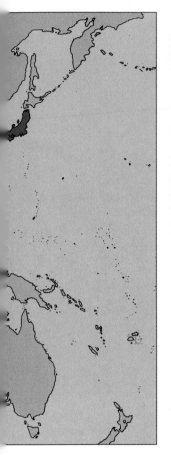

Konrad Wothe/Oxford Scientific Films

Mike Birkhead/Oxford Scientific Films

Most guenons live in forests, but the patas monkey has become a fast-running grassland specialist.

plateau of Ethiopia. Here, at 7,000–14,500 ft (2,000–4,400 m) above sea level, they survive on a diet that is 90 percent grass—indeed, they are the only true grazing primates. They have acquired dense fur as protection against the cold and developed habits that, once again, limit the amount of energy they expend on nonessential activities. With an abundant food source they rarely have to move far, saving energy by feeding from a sitting posture and generally staying within a few hundred yards of their sleeping sites in rocky cliff faces.

Conditions in the West African tropical forests are luxurious by comparison. A wide variety of foods are available throughout the year, and the three-dimensional structure of the forest may permit up to nine species of primates to thrive in the same area. Guenons in particular may forage together in multispecies groups, feeding in the upper layers of the canopy and drinking from small pools of water that collect in tree hollows and on the leaves of ferns and orchids. Since each species has slightly different requirements, they do not compete for food or space, and the group-living habit provides enhanced protection against deadly enemies such as eagles and venomous snakes. ∎

SOCIAL STRUCTURE

In most Old World monkey species, the females spend their lives in the group into which they were born. Males may come and go, but the social core of the group remains essentially female. Within the group the females form a dominance hierarchy, with each animal's position being determined by the number of other females to whom she is prepared to submit. Her daughters will also outrank the females (and their offspring) to whom their mother is dominant, although they will rank below her until she dies.

Mother and daughters stick together, forming a stable female kinship group called a matriline. The sisters support each other in disputes with other females and look after each other's offspring, acting (literally) as aunts. They sit together, move together, and groom each other assiduously. This acts as an expression of solidarity because the groomer is expending time and energy on her task, and in a subsistence economy like that of the monkeys, the expenditure of such valuable currency is a real sign of devotion.

Grooming has other functions. It can be a cleaning operation, involving the removal of dead skin, snagged vegetation, and burrs. It is not often the defleaing operation commonly imagined, although ticks may be a problem; if either are found they are promptly eaten. The other tidbit provided by grooming is salt. A rare and valuable commodity in the animal world, the flakes of salt from evaporated sweat are a prized reward for a groomer. The lip-smacking sound often made when a monkey has just eaten something it relishes has become part of the ritualized language of appeasement in some species, for since it is normally heard in a pleasant situation—grooming—it can be used to calm a potentially dangerous situation—much as a human will use a soft voice.

Adult male monkeys are generally larger than females and are dominant to them. They also have a hierarchy of their own, but it is much less stable

M. C. Wilkes/Aquila

Illustrations Guy Troughton/Wildlife Art Agency

TROOP TACTICS

Baboons normally travel in troops with the subordinate males at front and rear (right), *but if they encounter an enemy* (far right) *the dominant males face up to the threat while the other baboons beat a retreat.*

Playing together (left) *builds hierarchies, cements social bonds, and oils the wheels of monkey society. It also teaches the young monkeys something about life.*

MATRILINES

Among olive baboons (below) *the females form the core of the troop, reinforcing their social bonds by devoted grooming. A strange male must work hard to gain acceptance.*

ⓘⓝ SIGHT

WHOOP CALLS

Adult male gray-cheeked mangabeys have a distinctive territorial call; a low-pitched "whoop" followed by four to five seconds' silence, then a series of staccato "gobbling" noises. The pattern is not accidental, for the low-frequency whooping sound punches through the vegetation, so the call travels for a few miles, helping to space the mangabey troops through the forest. Meanwhile the gobble contains a sound code that identifies each male individually.

than that of the females. This is largely because males do not stay in the group into which they are born, and on arriving in a new group a male must work to attain social status, with its benefits of privileged access to food and females.

This involves both diplomacy and strength. An "immigrant" male olive baboon, for example, may spend months cultivating a relationship with a resident female, not simply to win her as a mate but to qualify as an accepted member of the troop. If he succeeds in establishing a bond with one female, he may be adopted into her immediate social network, and this will strengthen his position within the troop. A well-established male may make up to six close female "friends" like this. For their part the females benefit from the male's strength and his concern for the welfare of their young: A friendly male olive baboon will often defend an infant from predators or other troop members, even though he is not the father. For his part the male may hope to ingratiate himself to the infant's mother and get the opportunity to mate with her at a later date.

Meanwhile, he may have to compete against rival males, and despite the variety of ritualized signals for alleviating aggression, fights between males are common. These may be fatal, for males fight with their long, sharp canine teeth, which are quite capable of inflicting mortal wounds.

THE FORAGING MACHINE

The size of any monkey troop is limited by its food resources, and where food is scarce a large troop may subdivide into smaller troops, typically along matrilines. Each troop forages over a well-defined territory, and among guenons such as the blue monkey it is the females—the social core of the troop—that police the boundaries of the common territory and drive away intruders. Male blue monkeys do not engage in such disputes, for they rarely

BOSS MALES

Gaping in threat to display their fearsome canine teeth, rival hamadryas males dispute mastery of a harem while females and young males look on.

forage with a single troop for long and therefore have no vested interest in maintaining an exclusive territory.

HAMADRYAS SOCIETY

Female blue monkeys are unusually territorial, but the pattern of matriarchal society that they exemplify is typical of all Old World monkeys except one: the hamadryas baboon. Uniquely, this large ground-dwelling species has developed a social structure organized along patrilineal lines, in which the young males stay within their natal group, while the females are transient. The movement of females between groups reduces the inbreeding that might otherwise result if, like their brothers, young females were to stay in the group in which they were born. In other species the movement of males achieves the same end.

The hamadryas baboon lives in arid areas where food is sparse, and it has developed a unique four-tiered society that permits the effective exploitation of an environment where food resources are dispersed and sleeping sites are scarce.

The largest social unit is the troop: all the animals that sleep on a particular cliff. The troop size depends on the amount of sleeping space available, but a troop from a large cliff can number up to 750 animals. Every morning the troop breaks up into bands of animals that all head out in the same direction to forage. There are two or three bands in a troop, and each band is a permanent association of animals. Within a band, however, there

FACIAL EXPRESSIONS

Monkeys are highly visual creatures, and facial expressions are an important means of communication. Their meaning varies slightly between species, but most would recognize the open-mouthed threat (top left), a male's aggressive "yawning" display of his long canine teeth (top right), and the submissive fear grin (lower right). These signals are backed up by expressive body language to make their meaning absolutely clear.

Mutual grooming (right) *is important to rhesus macaques, cementing social ties within the group.*

Illustration John Cox/Wildlife Art Agency

Belinda Wright/Oxford Scientific Films

(in)SIGHT

BABY BONDING

If it is threatened by a dominant male, a subordinate male barbary macaque picks up a baby and presents it to its tormentor. Immediately the dominant male stops threatening and joins the other in cooing over the baby. Similar behavior occurs among other macaques and baboons, but in the barbary macaque it has become part of a ritualized "huddling" behavior used by males to reduce tension and promote social bonding. Its effectiveness can be seen in the fact that there may be up to ten adult males in a troop. In the past barbary macaques suffered badly from predation by big cats, and this may have stimulated the evolution of a social system in which many protective males are present.

are distinct subgroups called clans. These each consist of three to five harems, the basic units of hamadryas society.

A harem, which may comprise up to ten females and their young, is led on its daily food foray by a single male. The male asserts his authority over the females by force, in sharp contrast to the appeasing attitude adopted by the males of other species, and typically maintains his position for several years. In other Old World monkeys, associations between males and females are relatively brief, and the matri-line is the permanent social unit.

Sexual competition between rival males is particularly intense among hamadryas baboons, and since such rivalry tends to favor the evolution of powerful, imposing males, the difference in size between the sexes is the greatest of any primate: a 44-lb (20-kg) boss male is up to twice the size of an adult female. The difference is emphasized by the dramatic mane grown by a harem master. This grows with his status, since it is smaller in males without harems, and if a male loses his harem in a fight he may lose his mane and even, in extreme cases, grow fur with female coloration. ∎

FOOD AND FEEDING

Finding enough to eat can be tough even in the Tropics, so monkeys have evolved ways to do it with the minimum expenditure of energy.

One important development has been the perfection of color vision. For species that eat a lot of fruit, the ability to discriminate shades of color may be vital. A wrong choice based on poor color identification can mean wasted time or even, since many unripe fruits are protected with toxic chemicals, accidental poisoning. The sense of taste in many primates is also acute; monkeys can detect tiny amounts of toxins and have a sensitivity to sugar that allows a precise assessment of ripeness.

But it is not only the ripeness of an item that must be considered. To get the maximum energy yield for minimum energy expenditure, a foraging primate must reduce the search time and the time taken to handle, process, and digest any food item. Plants have evolved ways to protect their seeds, leaves, and roots, making them hard to open, difficult to find, or toxic or unpleasant. Some seeds contain high levels of tannins—chemicals that latch on to proteins when they are liberated from a bitten plant cell and render them indigestible. Because this so effectively reduces the nutritional value of food items, primates are sensitive to tannins and can taste them at very low concentrations.

Animals get into the swing of foraging for a particular food, so it is often efficient to exploit that food exclusively until it becomes so uncommon that it is no longer worth looking for. This explains why, when a swarm of locusts comes down, a generalist forager like a baboon will cease to feed on anything but locusts until the swarm moves on.

FAST AND FRUITY

But there is more to feeding than simply eating one's fill. Since any food item stays in the stomach for a given length of time while it is being digested, food selection involves a trade-off between readily available but bulky items such as leaves that yield energy slowly, and smaller, higher-value food items such as fruits that may be harder to find.

Compared to most fruit, leaves take longer to pass through the monkey. A long passage time gives the intestines longer to extract the nutrients from the food, but this time is limited by the daily energy needs of the animal. Bigger monkeys have a lower metabolic rate and can therefore afford a longer passage time; they also have a bigger body space to accommodate long guts. This allows the large baboons, for example, to feed heavily on grasses. In contrast, small species such as the talapoin have to search out high-energy fruits and insects.

For two similar-sized species, the one that eats fruits will be more active. Fruits shed their energy into the animal rapidly, and the fast passage time (three to five hours) soon relieves the guts for the next meal. But a leaf-eater, with guts full of slowly digesting leaves, has a passage time of around 50 hours, which limits the energy available to it. It lives life at a more relaxed pace, but it can do so because its food is just a hand's stretch away.

Getting enough protein is a problem for many primates. Smaller ones tend to solve it by eating insects, but in the larger species the solution may involve scavenging or active hunting. Some coastal populations of baboons and macaques will search the seashore for dead fish, but others living inland will raid birds' nests, dig out burrowing rodents, or even hunt down and kill small gazelles. ■

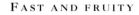

FRUITFUL DIET

Like many of the smaller species, the patas monkey (below) feeds mainly on high-value foods such as fruit, which can be hard to find but is relatively quick and easy to digest.

FISHING MONKEY

Allen's swamp monkey (left) is one of several species that has learned how to catch fish, a valuable source of protein. Other, less skilled monkeys may scavenge dead fish from the riverbank, and monkey troops living on the coast take crabs and other shellfish from the shore.

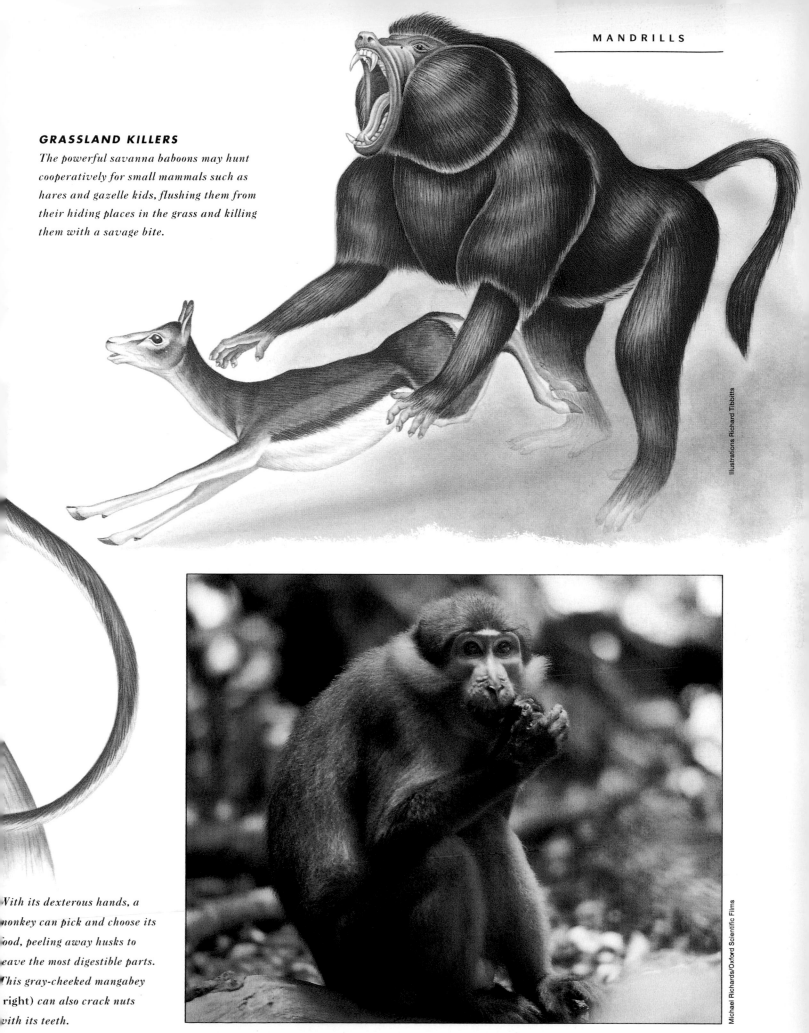

GRASSLAND KILLERS

The powerful savanna baboons may hunt cooperatively for small mammals such as hares and gazelle kids, flushing them from their hiding places in the grass and killing them with a savage bite.

With its dexterous hands, a monkey can pick and choose its food, peeling away husks to leave the most digestible parts. This gray-cheeked mangabey (right) can also crack nuts with its teeth.

Illustrations Richard Tibbitts

Michael Richards/Oxford Scientific Films

LIFE CYCLE

Old World monkeys breed slowly, with each long-lived female producing a single offspring at a time and investing a lot of time and energy in its care. This is partly because intelligence and learning are so important to these advanced primates, and each young animal needs individual attention. Most species also take several years to reach reproductive maturity. Female barbary macaques do not breed until they are around four years old, while a female talapoin, smallest of the guenons, takes some five to six years. Males mature at much the same age, but social constraints keep them from mating until they are several years older.

Most species mate during a limited breeding season that is typically defined by the climate: In most regions there are periods when the weather is favorable or food is particularly abundant, enabling

GROWING UP

The life of a barbary macaque

MATING

Mating is normally brief, lasting only a few seconds, but may happen several times while the female is in her fertile period.

HAIRY TRANSPORTATION

When the troop moves fast, or simply when the offspring is tired, the young infant will cling to its mother's belly fur and hitch a ride (below). Eventually it rides on her back, progressing to running alongside by twelve to fourteen months.

A TOKEN OF AFFECTION

Unusual for primates, male barbary macaques are not only interested in babies, but will actively play with them and groom them (above).

Illustrations Robin Budden/Wildlife Art Agency

Photo Reser/ZEFA

The birth is timed to coincide with a season of abundant food, since suckling (above) *makes great demands on the female's system.*

the mother to maintain a good supply of milk. Lactation can drain up to a third of an adult female's energy, and such a big investment would not be possible in adverse conditions.

In many species a female who is ready to conceive develops a swelling on the naked skin of her rump. This advertises her state, and she then becomes an object of intense interest to the males of her group. Among barbary macaques there is generally one dominant male to a group, and he is usually the first to take advantage of the situation; the female is not his "property," however

BORN IN A TREE

After a gestation of some seven and a half months, the female gives birth to a single infant. Because both mother and young are vulnerable to predators at this time, the birth normally occurs at night, in a tree (left). *The female descends at dawn with the infant clinging to her fur and rejoins the troop.*

FROM BIRTH TO DEATH

RHESUS MACAQUE
GESTATION: 135–194 DAYS (AVERAGE 166)
LITTER SIZE: 1, OCCASIONALLY 2
BREEDING: VARIABLE DEPENDING ON SEASONAL PATTERN OF HABITAT
WEIGHT AT BIRTH: 16 OZ (450 G)
EYES OPEN: IMMEDIATELY
FIRST WALKING: 4–5 WEEKS
WEANING: ABOUT 12 MONTHS
SEXUAL MATURITY: 3–4 YEARS IN FEMALE; 2–3 YEARS LATER IN MALES OWING TO SOCIAL CONSTRAINTS
LONGEVITY: 5–10 YEARS IN WILD, UP TO 35 YEARS IN CAPTIVITY

(unlike a harem female in a troop of hamadryas baboons), and she will actively seek out and mate with several males during her fertile period. This means that, as in many other species, the males are unable to monopolize particular females and cannot be sure that they have fathered their young. The male compensates for this by mating several times with a receptive female in attempt to flood her system with his sperm and, with luck, overwhelm that of any rivals.

The single young is born after a gestation of five to six months, usually at night in the mother's sleeping tree. Denied the comfort of a nursery, its first instinct is to cling to its mother's fur with her nipple in its mouth. It is nursed like this for several months, gradually becoming more independent and inquisitive until it is fully weaned. By the time its mother is pregnant again, the young monkey is capable of foraging for itself, but it will live and feed alongside its mother, watching and learning, for several years until the onset of sexual maturity turns its attention to other matters. ■

in SIGHT

PATERNAL CARE

Unusual for monkeys, male barbary macaques fulfill a number of "maternal" duties. Starting only a few days after an infant is born, a male will carry, groom, and play with it. An adult male intent on child care makes a special facial expression, drawing back his lips and the corners of his mouth and chattering his bared teeth. This probably indicates that he means no harm, although in other macaques it is a gesture of submission. Recent work has suggested that the males may choose particular infants to care for, since if a male takes care of a female's offspring by another male she is more likely to mate with him the next time around.

PRIMATES IN PERIL

THROUGHOUT THEIR RANGE THE OLD WORLD PRIMATES ARE UNDER INCREASING PRESSURE FROM HABITAT DESTRUCTION, HUNTING FOR MEAT AND MEDICINE, AND CAPTURE FOR SCIENTIFIC RESEARCH

Visit virtually any village market in central and West Africa to browse among the plantains, yams, and other village produce and you could stumble across a nightmare vision: a heap of blackened corpses, their eyes shriveled in their sockets, their shrunken lips stretched taut to bare their teeth in a hideous grin of death. They could be the victims of some political atrocity, but they are too small to be human. They are monkeys, shot in the forest, smoked whole, and brought to market to be sold for food: bush meat.

There is a long tradition of eating wild game in Africa; indeed, many tribal people still live as hunter-gatherers in much the same way as their prehistoric ancestors. In parts of Africa, wild-caught meat is the second most important source of local protein after fish, which is also taken from the wild in a form of hunting, and not just by tribal Africans. To a certain extent, conservationists are in favor of this traditional way of life since it relies on the preservation of wild animals in their habitats and does not involve the destruction of forests and wild grasslands for agriculture. But in the modern Africa, where wild animals are already under pressure from such environmental degradation, persistent hunting for bush meat can be a major factor in the decline of rare species, and this is particularly true in the case of the primates.

Monkey meat might seem an unlikely delicacy, but it is highly prized in many parts of Africa. Monkey hunting for food is uncommon in Asia, where the proscriptions of Buddhism and Hinduism protect them, and African Muslims will not harm monkeys either. Africans of other religions—both traditional and Christian—have no such inhibitions, however, and monkey hunting is common, especially in West Africa where the animals are taken both for home consumption and for

Martin Harvey/NHPA

Dancing monkeys in India (above)—just two of the many thousands captured and sold each year.

the market stall. Some traditional medicines also use parts of monkeys. Only the tiniest species, such as the talapoin, are considered worthless for food, and heavy hunting has endangered several species that are found only in West Africa, such as the drill in Equatorial Guinea and the white-thoated guenon in Nigeria. The smokey mangabey is widely hunted for food, making it rare in western Nigeria and Gabon, and in some places it is also punitively hunted because it raids the crops of local farmers. Some countries such as Liberia have been almost

For every monkey that learns to dance or becomes a pet, many die of neglect in squalid cages.

Mike Hill/Oxford Scientific Films

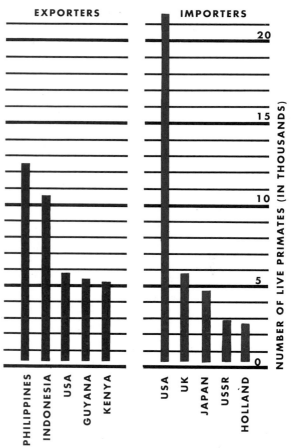

This graph shows the world's top traders in live primates; figures given are for 1986.

EXPORTERS | IMPORTERS

NUMBER OF LIVE PRIMATES (IN THOUSANDS)

20

15

10

5

0

PHILIPPINES · INDONESIA · USA · GUYANA · KENYA

USA · UK · JAPAN · USSR · HOLLAND

These figures, compiled by CITES, reveal that the West is still the major importer of live primates. The total trade figure for 1986 amounted to 51,000 live animals— and these were legal exports; many more were probably traded illegally.

hunted out, and dead monkeys are now being imported from neighboring Sierra Leone to meet the continuing demand for monkey flesh.

The monkeys that end up in the cooking pot are only part of the problem. Originally the animals were hunted with bows and arrows, snares, and traps, but today most hunters prefer to use shotguns. Shotgun cartridges manufactured in the Congo Republic are widely available throughout the region, but the guns themselves are expensive; consequently the hunters make their own rudimentary versions that lack the refinements designed to increase accuracy and concentrate the shot on the target. This means they work like the sawed-off shotguns used by bank robbers, scattering shot over a broad area at every discharge. It also reduces their lethal effect, yet while this may comfort a potential victim of a bank robbery it is disastrous for the monkeys of the African forests, which cannot check into their local hospital to have the pellets removed. The wounds fester, eventually maiming and killing several monkeys for every one that falls dead to be gathered up by the hunter.

LIMITATIONS OF HABITAT

Around half of Africa's monkeys are threatened in some way, either by hunting or habitat destruction. Of these, seven are considered to be "vulnerable," and six "endangered," while two are considered naturally rare. Generalist species like the red-bellied guenon are mainly threatened by hunting, but habitat erosion, and deforestation in particular, threatens habitat specialists such as the bamboo-loving owl-faced monkey and L'Hoest's monkey, an inhabitant of dense montane forests on the borders of Zaire and Uganda. Such species are unable to adapt to the alterations that follow deforestation, and generally disappear from the area even if there is a regrowth of secondary forest.

The diana monkey is an example of a species that, while widespread in West Africa, is limited by its diet and therefore vulnerable to habitat loss. Although able to survive in lightly logged areas, its reliance on the upper canopy as a source of fruits and oil-rich seeds means that it is unable to exploit

---

DEAD MONKEYS ARE BEING IMPORTED INTO LIBERIA FROM SIERRA LEONE TO MEET THE DEMAND FOR MONKEY MEAT

---

the secondary forest and scrub that may eventually grow on the land after heavy logging. Because of this, diana monkeys are useful indicators of pristine habitats and are used as such by scientists when surveying areas for conservation importance.

Logging is itself intimately bound up with the bush meat problem. The hunters hitch rides on the logging vehicles to reach new hunting grounds, and they may even establish thriving villages that subsist entirely on the profits of the hunt in the cleared areas. They do not have to look far to find a market, since the logging companies employ mainly local people who are only too willing to live on a diet of bush meat while they take out the timber.

Some of the most endangered monkeys are those with very small ranges and slow reproductive rates. The Tana River mangabey, or agile mangabey, is confined to small areas of seasonally flooded forest alongside the Tana River in Kenya, and its population is thought to be less than 1,100 individuals. Its reproductive rate is also relatively

ENDANGERED SPECIES

VICTIMS OF RESEARCH

Monkeys have been used in scientific research for centuries. In the Middle Ages physicians were forbidden to dissect human corpses, so they learned about anatomy by examining dead monkeys instead. More recently a similar attitude prompted the widespread use of live monkeys in research into human disease prevention and psychological processes, employing procedures that often involved a degree of pain and a detailed autopsy. This meant that there was a regular demand for research animals, and suppliers were not hard to find.

Imports of live wild-collected primates peaked in the 1950s as scientists searched for a vaccine for polio. The United States was the major importer of primates for such medical use: in the late 1950s it imported 200,000 primates a year. Although a lot of South American animals were used, many were obtained from Africa and Asia, with the rhesus macaque bearing the brunt of the trade. These figures masked the many thousands of animals that died before being exported, and the trade almost completely denuded some areas of their monkeys.

The techniques learned from these animals led to scientific advances that reduced the need for primates in medical research. Consequently, collecting live animals from the wild for laboratories has diminished in recent years since the

CONSERVATION MEASURES

● At one time up to 70 percent of a consignment of live monkeys could die in transit. To reduce this loss there are now strict rules governing the conditions under which live primates may be shipped. Many airlines now refuse to carry them at all.

● In 1984 Malaysia banned all exports of live primates to laboratories. This example has been followed by many other countries.

boratories need fewer animals and any now breed their own. Currently, the orld trade in wild-caught primates for edical research is estimated to be in the gion of 15,000–20,000 annually.

Compared to this, the number of Old orld monkeys sold as pets and for street ntertainment is negligible, but the trade eeds to be stopped, because it encourges a patronizing attitude to the animals, hich can only hinder conservation. The eatment of wild animals as mere com-odities has to be discouraged if their ght to survival is to be upheld.

EDICAL RESEARCH HAS GAINED INVALUABLE NSIGHT FROM PRIMATE SUBJECTS BUT NOW EEKS TO AVOID THEIR USE AS MUCH AS POSSIBLE.

Inset picture David Hiser/Tony Stone Worldwide

The year 1975 saw the establishment f the Convention on the nternational Trade in Endangered pecies (CITES). The aim of CITES was to regulate the trade n rare species, in living animals estined for laboratories, zoos, nd private collections, and in urios, souvenirs, and gifts made rom them. Today CITES has ver 120 member countries and s a major force in primate onservation.

MONKEYS IN DANGER

ALL SPECIES ARE DECLINING TO A GREATER OR LESSER DEGREE AND ARE GIVEN PROTECTION ACROSS MOST OF THEIR RANGE. THESE ARE JUST A FEW OF THE DOZENS LISTED IN THE *RED DATA BOOK*:

MANDRILL	VULNERABLE
JAPANESE MACAQUE	VULNERABLE
DIANA MONKEY	VULNERABLE
L'HOEST'S MONKEY	VULNERABLE
DRILL	ENDANGERED
RED-BELLIED GUENON	ENDANGERED
WHITE-THROATED GUENON	ENDANGERED
SUN-TAILED GUENON	ENDANGERED
PREUSS'S GUENON	ENDANGERED
LION-TAILED MACAQUE	ENDANGERED

low, since females take four to five years to reach sexual maturity and the interbirth interval for the single infants is between eighteen months and two years. This means that a population is slow to recover if it is disturbed or hunted. One of the major threats to the survival of this species is the felling of large trees for dugout canoes, since this deprives it of both food and shelter.

Species such as gelada and hamadryas baboons are naturally rare. The gelada is found only in the central highlands of Ethiopia, which is also the main home for the hamadryas. Occurring only on montane grasslands, where it feeds almost exclusively on grasses, the gelada faces heavy competition for grazing from domestic goats and cattle and may be suffering as a result. However, the region's long-running civil war has made information on the status of this specialized animal difficult to obtain.

Meanwhile, the future of the hamadryas in some areas is threatened by conflict with farmers. Its preference for dry areas used to keep it out of harm's way, but recent development programs have used irrigation schemes to convert semiarid marginal terrain into land suitable for agriculture. The hamadryas troops, forever opportunistic, feast on the crops, and are shot for their pains. A subtler threat to the hamadryas is hybridization with its

OUT OF ACTION

INSIDIOUS ENEMIES

Some parasitic flies lay eggs in the nostrils of monkeys. When the maggots hatch, they slide down the monkey's throat and settle in its stomach, where they burrow into the stomach lining to feed. Eventually they are excreted and pupate, to emerge as adult flies ready to lay more eggs. Another variety lays its eggs on the monkey's tail. The hatching maggots then burrow into their host's flesh and live on its blood. Before pupating the maggots can reach 0.5 in (4 cm) long and cause serious damage.

Some monkeys have their own viruses to which they are immune but which can kill humans. An example is the green monkey virus, which, although named after the green monkey, or vervet, occurs in a number of West African species. The fact that many monkeys suffer from diseases contagious to humans is one reason they are used for medical research.

Monkeys that live in cold habitats can suffer from frostbite, a problem that normally affects the tail, which has unusually poor blood circulation. This may be the reason that several macaques found in cold climates, such as the barbary and Japanese macaque, have only short tails or have lost them altogether.

Kevin Schaffer/NHPA

Larger forest-dwellers like the mandrill (above) *need space, and are hard hit by deforestation.*

close relative the olive baboon. In the past the two species were kept apart by their preferences for different habitats, but recent disruption of their environment has brought them into close contact, resulting in a degree of crossbreeding that not only adulterates the species but also introduces a disruptive element into the network of relationships that make up hamadryas society.

For some species lack of knowledge has been one of the main barriers to conservation. Sclater's guenon is one of Africa's rarest and least-known monkeys. Found only in the rain forest zone of southern Nigeria, between the Niger and Cross Rivers, it was known only from four museum skins and an unpublished field observation. Occurring in an area of high human population density that has lost most of its natural forest, it was once thought to be extremely rare and in imminent danger of extinction. Happily, field researchers have now found it in five forest patches. Although in many places it is threatened by tree-cutting and hunting, two of the forests are near villages of the Igbo tribe, who regard the monkey as a sacred animal. Conservationists are now working with the Igbo to ensure the monkey's continued survival. ∎

Zig Leszczynski/Oxford Scientific Films

The spectacular drill has been hunted to the brink of extinction in the forests of Equatorial Guinea.

INTO THE FUTURE

The future of the Old World monkeys is threatened first and foremost by increasing human population and loss of habitat. Trade in primates is increasingly under strict regulation.

In naturally forested areas, habitat destruction often begins with commercial logging. The short-term impact of such operations is dramatic, but the long-term effects can be equally damaging. For every commercially valuable tree extracted, up to twenty others may be damaged and ultimately killed. The remaining trees may be severely stressed and fail to produce the fruits and leaves the monkeys eat, and the monkeys themselves may be stressed, fail to breed, or move away entirely. The logging roads provide access for small farmers, who compound the damage with slash-and-burn agriculture, and even if the trees regrow, such secondary forest rarely provides suitable monkey habitat. The

PREDICTION

MACAQUE UNDER ATTACK

The lion-tailed macaque of southern India is one of the world's most endangered mammals. The largest wild population is threatened by road-building and a dam project, and since the other wild populations are too small for long-term viability, the species may be doomed.

rapid growth of human populations in Africa means that the demand for timber and land is unlikely to slow down, so the problem of habitat loss will grow.

Meanwhile the threats posed by collecting and hunting may be fading. Collecting for laboratories has diminished in recent years; laboratories have made a commitment to use fewer animals. Zoo collections have been put to conservation use not only in public education, but some zoo-bred primates are now being reintroduced to nature. Community education programs in Africa, where monkeys are still widely hunted, are beginning to have some impact, and local people are becoming more inclined to value their wildlife for its own sake—or as a valuable tourist attraction—than as potential bush meat. For species such as the drill and the white-throated guenon, which have been critically endangered by hunting, such changes in attitudes may make all the difference between survival and extinction. ■

THE PANDRILLUS DRILL

The drill is a heavily built forest-living baboon from Nigeria and Cameroon that, owing to habitat loss and hunting, is now one of Africa's rarest monkeys. Pandrillus, a conservation group set up in 1991, studies drills both in their natural habitats and in captivity. With funding from the Fauna and Flora Preservation Society and British Airways, the group is surveying wild drill populations; and with help from the Nigerian government and grants from Whitley Animal Protection Trust, Pandrillus has founded the Drill Rehabilitation and Breeding Center. This rescues illegally held drills, most of which are orphaned when their nursing mothers are shot for bush meat. The center now has some 20 drills, the world's largest captive group. Living in an 11-acre forested enclosure, they can forage, roam, and sleep as they would in the wild.

The center is also the focus of a village-based antipoaching and conservation education program. In 1994 the center had its first drill birth, a baby male named Mgbochi, and the arrival has given a tremendous boost to the center's education efforts. As one Nigerian visitor was heard to say, "That's not bush meat, that's a mother and child." The center hopes to build on this success and, eventually, reintroduce drills into the wild.

Illustration Kim Thompson

MARMOSET MONKEYS

RELATIONS

Marmosets and tamarins belong to the suborder Anthropoidea or higher primates. Other members of the suborder include:

CAPUCHINS

SAKIS

BABOONS

MACAQUES

CHIMPANZEES

GIBBONS

HUMAN

Kevin Schafer/NHPA

MINIATURE MONKEYS

COMMUNICATING IN PIPING SHRIEKS, MARMOSETS AND TAMARINS MAKE UP FOR THEIR TINY STATURE WITH THEIR SHEER EXUBERANCE. THEIR RESPLENDENT ATTIRE INCLUDES RUFFS, EAR TUFTS, AND MUSTACHES

Two families of primates occur in the Americas: marmosets and tamarins comprise the Callithricidae monkey family (the callithricids), and the capuchins, howler monkeys, woolly monkeys, sakis, and uakaris form the Cebidae family (the cebids). Marmosets and tamarins are very small monkeys that live in rain forest and scrubland habitats throughout Central and South America. They are social animals and live in small family groups.

Except for the mouse-lemurs, marmosets and tamarins are the smallest primates, with the marmosets being the smallest monkeys. They vary from mouse- to squirrel-sized. Their fur is soft, often silky, and many have furry tufts or ruffs on the head. Their furry tails are not prehensile like many primates', such as those of their cebid neighbors, so marmosets and tamarins do not swing through the branches. Instead, they scurry like squirrels.

The cotton-top tamarin (right) *is aptly named, with its shock of white hair framing its face.*

Most marmosets have a body length of about 8–10 in (20–25 cm) with a tail about 12 in (30 cm) long. The tiny pygmy marmoset has a body under 7.5 in (19 cm) long, with an 8-in (20-cm) tail; it is the smallest monkey in the world.

The common marmoset, from the Brazilian coastal forests, has silky fur marbled with black and gray, a black head, and long white tufts of hair around the ears. There are three or four closely related species from the Brazil coast as far south as the Paraguay border and the Amazon River Basin.

MARMOSETS ARE TERRITORIAL PRIMATES LIVING IN FAMILY GROUPS WITHIN THEIR DRY SCRUB AND RAIN FOREST HABITAT

The white-eared marmoset is one of the plumed species. Its small face has a pale, triangular blaze on the forehead and largish ears partly concealed by the plumelike hairs that sprout from its cheeks.

The Goeldi's marmoset, or Goeldi's monkey, is dark brown with a bushy mane of hair around its head and shoulders. It is highly vocal, communicating with a set of trills and whistles. The exact status of its population is uncertain, but it is known to be very rare and to have a patchy, localized distribution. The pygmy marmoset of the

Stephen Dalton/NHPA

Michael Dick/Oxford Scientific Films

The golden-headed lion tamarin lives in fragments of the forests on Brazil's eastern seaboard.

ANCESTORS

The New World monkeys first appear in the Oligocene record of South America, dating back some 35 million years. This is surprising, since at that time South America had already split from Africa, where their closest contemporary relatives have been found. One theory is that primitive primates may have floated over on debris from Central America, across the stretch of water that separated these landmasses during much of the Tertiary Period (65 to 2 million years ago).

upper Amazon (in Brazil, Peru, southern Colombia, and northern Bolivia) has no ear tufts and the hair of the head is swept back over the ears. It is brown, marbled with tawny, and has a banded tail. Pygmy marmosets live in troops of five to ten animals, in which the females are dominant.

The silvery marmoset lives in the forest and tall grass of Brazil and Bolivia. It is easily recognizable by its silky, silvery white body fur and the lack of hair on its face and ears, which are reddish. There is often some gray fur on its back, and its tail is black. It is one of the larger marmosets, having a body length of up to 12 in (30 cm) and a tail length of up to 15.5 in (40 cm).

THE TAMARINS

Tamarins live on the larger branches of trees at all levels in the South American forests, scaling the heights easily with the help of their long, curved claws. The tamarins usually weigh 9–21 oz

(250–600 g) and are about 6–14 in (15–35 cm) long, with a tail of 10–16 in (25–40 cm). They live in groups of between 6 and 24, with each group requiring up to about 100 acres (40 ha) of space.

The black-and-red tamarin of the Colombia-Ecuador-Brazil border is typical of its genus, with its short, broad hands equipped with claws, and a small body. It is marbled black on its foreparts and red-brown on its hind parts, with white hair around the mouth. The skin under the mustache is pigmented, as are the genitalia.

The black tamarin, found on both sides of the Amazon estuary, is black marbled with buff, with one subspecies having golden hands and feet. The closely related brown-headed tamarin varies in color but usually has a marbled saddle separating its reddish foreparts from the darker hind parts.

MARMOSETS AND TAMARINS LACK THE OPPOSABLE THUMB THAT IS TYPICAL OF OTHER MONKEYS—BUT THEY DO HAVE AN OPPOSABLE BIG TOE

The red-chested tamarin has a white mustache with pink skin beneath it and a black-brown back that contrasts with a red underside. Related to this are the yellow-brown mustached tamarin, on which the white hairs cover the lower part of the nose, and the fascinating emperor tamarin, which has a long, majestic handlebar mustache and is gray with a red tail.

Other tamarins have almost hairless faces. The pied tamarin has big, bare ears, whitish foreparts, and brown to black hind parts. The white-footed tamarin has a short crest on the forehead and is brownish gray with white hands and feet. The Pinché or cotton-top has a long crest like a warrior in full dress and is dark brown with a white belly and limbs.

LION TAMARINS

The lion tamarins from the drier, hardwood coastal forests of south and east Brazil are a little different in appearance. They are larger, with long, slim hands and feet and shorter tails, and have long, silky manes on the head. The golden lion tamarin is a beautiful red-gold; its bare face is a pinkish-purple skin color. It has large, round eyes and a somewhat pug nose.

The golden-headed lion tamarin is black with a golden mane and arms; the golden-rumped, or black, lion tamarin is black with a golden forehead and rump patch; and the black-faced lion tamarin is gold with black face, hands, and tail. ■

THE MARMOSETS' FAMILY TREE

Marmosets and tamarins, together with the cebid monkeys, are known as New World monkeys. They are in the suborder Anthropoidea (higher primates), which also includes the Old World monkeys, the apes, and humans. The higher primates, plus the species in the suborder Prosimii (lower primates such as lemurs, galagos, and tarsiers), form the fascinating order Primates.

COMMON MARMOSET
Callithrix jacchus
(CALL-i-thrix JACK-us)

The common marmoset has a general color of agouti gray and a tail that alternates with broad blackish and narrow pale bands. It has mostly white or grayish tufts of hair around its ears and a black or brown forehead and temples. It is found in eastern Brazil, including the coastal forest regions.

GOELDI'S MONKEY
Callimico goeldii
(Cal-IMM-i-co GOLD-ee-ie)

B/W illustrations Ruth Grewcock

OLD WORLD MONKE
APES, & HUMANS

PYGMY MARMOSET
Cebuella pygmaea
(Seb-yoo-ELL-a pig-MAY-a)

The only member of its genus, this is the smallest of the living monkeys; for some time it was thought to be a young form of another species. It weighs 2.5–6.5 oz (70–180 g), with an adult head-and-body length of 6.7–7 in (17–18 cm). A mane of long hair frames its face, and its tail is ringed.

GOLDEN LION TAMARIN
Leontopithecus rosalia
(Lee-ON-to-pith-ek-us ros-AL-ya)

MARMOSETS & TAMARINS
Callithricidae
(Call-i-TRICK-id-ie)

CAPUCHIN-LIKE MONKEYS
Cebidae
(SEB-id-ie)

NEW WORLD MONKEYS

COTTON-TOP TAMARIN
Saguinus oedipus
(Sa-GWIN-us EE-di-puss)

HIGHER PRIMATES

ANATOMY:
THE MARMOSET

Sizes range from the tiny pygmy marmoset, with a head-to-tail length of up to 15 in (39 cm) and a weight of 2.5–6 oz (70–180 g), to the lion tamarin with a head-to-tail length of 24–30 in (60–78 cm) and a weight of 22–32 oz (630–900 g). Most callithricids are about 18–30 in (45–75 cm) in total length and weigh 9–21 oz (250–600 g).

VERVET MONKEY

GOELDI'S MONKEY

THE MARMOSET'S EYES

are large and round. They point forward to give binocular vision that is good for judging distance. However, the monkey has limited binocular cortex areas in the brain, so it cocks its head from side to side to give more than one view of an object and provide more clues for the brain to use.

DIFFERENT NOSES

The callithricids, together with the monkeys of the Cebidae family, are known as the platyrrhine (PLAT-i-rine)—meaning flat-nosed—monkeys.

The Goeldi's nose (above right), like all platyrrhine monkeys, is very flat and broad, and the nostrils point sideways.

The Old World monkeys, such as the vervet (above left), have a narrower nose with nostrils that point downward.

ALL FOUR LEGS

are covered in fur and are strong for tree climbing. The forelimbs are shorter than the hind limbs.

MARMOSET SKELETON

The skeleton clearly shows the relative length of the head, body, and tail, with the tail doubling the overall length. The body is small with fine bones, giving great agility in the trees.

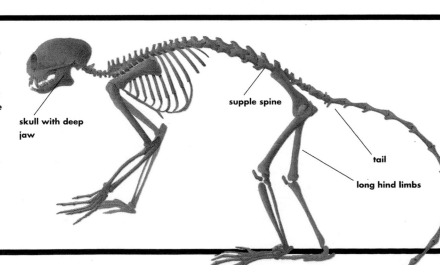

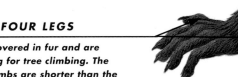

skull with deep jaw

supple spine

tail

long hind limbs

elbow joint

elongat[ed] fingers

long forearm

FOREARM/HAND

The fingers are very thin and elongated, clawed, and well adapted for probing tree-growing plants for insects. The thumb is not opposable (it cannot grasp).

FEET

FOREFOOT

The common marmoset's feet have toes that are all clawed except for the large toe on the hind foot, which bears a nail. The large toe is opposable.

large toe

HIND FOOT

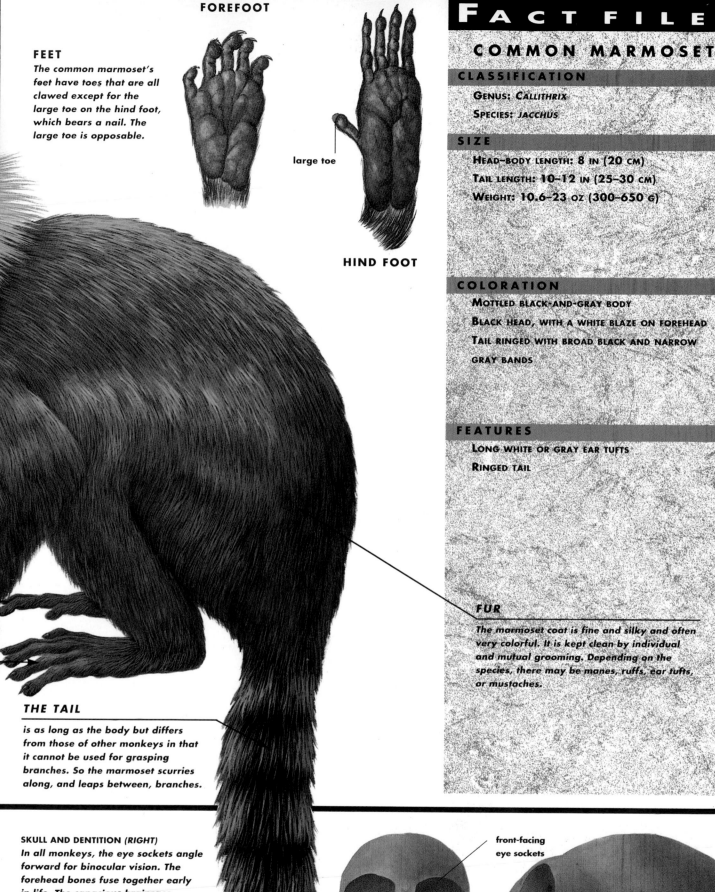

FACT FILE:

COMMON MARMOSET

CLASSIFICATION

GENUS: *CALLITHRIX*

SPECIES: *JACCHUS*

SIZE

HEAD–BODY LENGTH: 8 IN (20 CM)

TAIL LENGTH: 10–12 IN (25–30 CM)

WEIGHT: 10.6–23 OZ (300–650 G)

COLORATION

MOTTLED BLACK-AND-GRAY BODY

BLACK HEAD, WITH A WHITE BLAZE ON FOREHEAD

TAIL RINGED WITH BROAD BLACK AND NARROW GRAY BANDS

FEATURES

LONG WHITE OR GRAY EAR TUFTS

RINGED TAIL

FUR

The marmoset coat is fine and silky and often very colorful. It is kept clean by individual and mutual grooming. Depending on the species, there may be manes, ruffs, ear tufts, or mustaches.

THE TAIL

is as long as the body but differs from those of other monkeys in that it cannot be used for grasping branches. So the marmoset scurries along, and leaps between, branches.

SKULL AND DENTITION *(RIGHT)*
In all monkeys, the eye sockets angle forward for binocular vision. The forehead bones fuse together early in life. The capacious braincase reflects the relatively large brain size. The two halves of the lower jaw are fused at the midline. The body of the jaw is fairly deep.

Callithricid molars have three cusps (there are four cusps in other anthropoids). In marmosets, the lower incisors are as long as the canines.

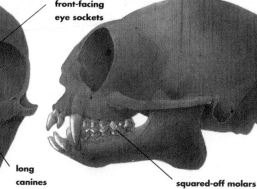

front-facing eye sockets

long canines

squared-off molars

AGILE AND AGGRESSIVE

SEEMINGLY AT ODDS WITH THEIR CUDDLY APPEARANCE, THESE TINY TREE-DWELLERS DO NOT HESITATE IN SHOWING THEIR DISPLEASURE, BRISTLING AND SHRIEKING WHEN ANOTHER INVADES THEIR TERRITORY

Marmosets and tamarins, being relatively lightweight, can reach the outermost branches of the forest trees. They are extremely active animals that bound or scurry along branches like squirrels, using jerky movements. Marmosets are agile leapers, while tamarins and pygmy marmosets move more vertically through the trees. Unlike many other primates, marmosets and tamarins lack an opposable (grasping, pincerlike) thumb, so they cannot readily grip branches or manipulate objects.

Family groups, usually comprising a mated pair and its offspring, live mainly in the upper forest canopy. The cotton-top tamarin has been observed sleeping in broad tree forks, after entering the tree in the late afternoon, and then rising and moving about an hour after dawn. The black tamarin, on the other hand, feeds at lower levels

A female tassel-eared marmoset in the Amazon rain forests of Brazil (above).

> **BLACK TAMARINS HAVE BEEN REPORTED LEAPING 49 FT (15 M) FROM THE TOP OF A TREE TO THE GROUND WITHOUT INJURY**

and climbs into the thicker foliage of taller trees in the heat of the day. This species has been seen to leap 26 ft (8 m) horizontally, losing an equivalent distance in height, but the cotton-top and the pied tamarin do not leap.

Marmosets and tamarins spend much of their day feeding busily. As well as eating insects, leaves, and fruit, many species—marmosets in particular—gnaw tree bark with their specialized front teeth and suck out the sap or gum. This leaves a hole in the tree, which they mark with urine and scent from a genital gland. They defend these holes over an area of 2.5 acres (1 ha). Tamarins, however, have a larger territory of up to 12.5 acres (5 ha), probably because of their more varied food needs.

It is not certain that marmoset and tamarin family pairs are completely territorial, but much of their behavior, such as marking, indicates that they are. Some studies of captive marmosets have found that two members of the same sex will fight if caged together. Also, when two male marmosets meet in the wild, they threaten each other. They walk near each other with backs arched, pulling back the corners of the mouth and rapidly lowering and raising their white ear tufts as aggressive signals.

Marmosets and tamarins use a range of facial expressions, including grimacing and raising their eyebrows, to threaten their rivals or enemies or to

A Geoffroy's marmoset having a meal of fruit in the Atlantic rain forest of Espirito Santo State, in southeast Brazil (right).

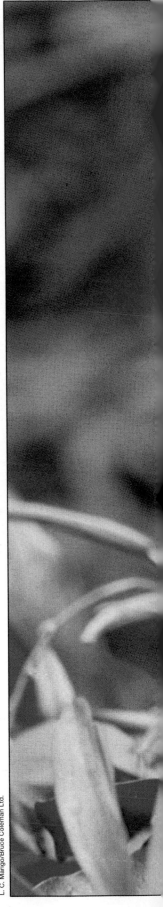

express their feelings or intentions. The golden lion tamarin is highly aggressive toward intruders, and if startled it erects its mane, bares its teeth, and emits high-pitched shrills and shrieks.

Other general offensive threat postures include arching the back (the "arch-bristle," often used within the group) and presenting the rump with tail raised (often used between members of different groups).

WHEN HIGHLY AGITATED, MARMOSETS AND TAMARINS STAND UPRIGHT ON THEIR HIND FEET

In 1991, Japanese researchers found that young common marmosets show a left- or right-hand preference, just like humans. Until then, this phenomenon had been known in no other mammal besides man. The researchers conducted a detailed study of 23 marmoset families and noted which hand the animals used to pick up pieces of food. They found that 43 percent of the adults were left-handed, 24 percent were right-handed, and 33 percent were ambidextrous. They discovered that, far from being a random choice, the favored hand of an infant marmoset strongly correlates with that of its mother, as in humans, even though it is the father that provides most of the youngster's early care. The trait is probably passed down through the mother's genes. ∎

Goeldi's monkey (below) *has been seriously depleted by illegal trapping and habitat loss.*

HABITATS

The Callithricidae monkeys live in a mixture of scrubland and rain forest areas in Central and South America. The Amazonian rain forest is probably the most exciting because it is like a hothouse world inhabited by a vast variety of birds, mammals, and insects. It is a threatened paradise that we have really only just started to explore. It is also of fundamental importance to the balance of the earth's atmosphere, because its trees are the largest oxygen producers on the earth's surface.

The rain forest contains about two-thirds of the world's freshwater, including the Amazon River and over 1,000 tributaries. It covers more than a third of South America and has over half the world's plant and animal species living in it. Within the Amazon Basin there are several hundred species of monkesy, more than 600 bird species, and over 40,000 species of flowering plants. Also, the vegetation supports millions of insects; 20,000 species can inhabit an area the size of a football field. Particularly in moist tropical rain forests, insects, amphibians, and fish have all developed unique, specialized lifestyles. This variation is partly due to South America's unusual geological history. The

---

THE UPPER AMAZON REGION CONTAINS THE GREATEST VARIETY OF TAMARIN AND MARMOSET SPECIES

---

fragmentation of the continents over 100 million years ago meant that its animals evolved in isolation for millions of years until the creation of the land bridge with North America, about 3.5 million years ago, allowed other species to enter.

SPECIES UNDER THREAT

This amazing diversity is only a part of an even greater variety spread across South America. There are about 800 mammal species and 3,000 bird species in South America, 80 percent of which are unique to the region. These bird species account for one-third of the world's total. Some 70 mammal, 300 bird, and over 80 other species are threatened. Surprisingly, only four mammal and two bird species are thought to have become extinct since 1600, including the glaucous macaw, Colombian grebe, and Falkland Islands wolf. Notable threatened endemic species, other than marmosets and tamarins, include the woolly spider monkey, maned wolf, giant otter, little blue macaw, South American river turtle, and the Galapagos land snail.

DISTRIBUTION

The various species of marmosets and tamarins inhabit different areas of the upper Amazon, but the family as a whole covers Columbia, Brazil, Bolivia, Peru, northern Paraguay, and Panama.

KEY

MARMOSETS & TAMARINS ■

Michael Freeman/Bruce Coleman Ltd.

Plants have adapted well to the rain forest environment, where there is plenty of heat and humidity. The tree canopy forms a layer 33 ft (10 m) deep, which captures about 95 percent of the available sunlight. Liana vines and other creepers struggle to reach this level to flower. Giant trees grow throughout the forest and most of these flower brilliantly, later producing fruit for fruit-eating creatures like the marmosets and tamarins, the cebid monkeys, and the fruit bats. A lot of the seeds from

---

BUSHY TREE GROWTH AND THICK TANGLES OF LIANA VINES PROVIDE GOOD SLEEPING SITES FOR THESE MONKEYS

---

the canopy level never reach the ground, but germinate in the moist cushion of debris and tree-living plants high above the ground. Ferns, large orchids, and bromeliad plants are epiphytes—plants that live high up on other trees, where they receive the light and water they need. The bromeliads collect rainwater and insects in cup-forming leaves, which provide them with both moisture and nutrients. Their sticky seeds are carried by birds to other trees where they germinate and grow.

There is an enormous population of platyrrhine (flat-nosed) monkeys in the forest canopy, and much of the large volume of dung that they produce is caught on the branches of the canopy. There it is disassembled rapidly by droves of dung

L. C. Marigo/Bruce Coleman Ltd.

The Geoffroy's tufted-ear or white-faced marmoset (above).

A pygmy marmoset (left) perches on grasses, easily justifying its status as the world's smallest monkey.

KEY FACTS

● **The combined mass of all the tropical moist forests—Amazonia included—accounts for 80 percent of the earth's vegetation, even though they occupy no more than 7 percent of the planet's surface.**

● **The endangered buffy-headed marmoset survives only in Atlantic forest remnants in southeast Brazil.**

● **The Goeldi's marmoset is rare throughout its range, but especially so in parts of Colombia where the slash-and-burn style of agriculture has destroyed much of its habitat.**

● **The rain forest's soil is surprisingly poor in nutrients, tending instead to be thin and sandy. The organic debris that falls to the ground simply does not get a chance to leach into the soil, because it is recycled so quickly by the forest's flora and fauna. For this reason, most attempts to graze cattle or grow crops on cleared rain forest land fail within a couple of years, when the nutritive value of the land peters out.**

beetles. Millions of ants and termites devour any decaying logs, leaves, or corpses of other animals. These and other insects are eaten by marmosets and tamarins. The canopy provides a complete food chain, with monkeys, tree-climbing rats and mice, sloths, birds, and insects feeding on fruits and seeds, and in turn becoming food for other animals. Spiders, too, feed on small invertebrates—and they themselves fall prey to the monkeys.

LIVING IN A PERFECT NICHE

The tropical rain forests provide a rich and varied environment, and the animals living in this hot-house environment have specialized to fill every tiny habitat type and to exploit every possible food source. Yet some ancient species have survived from before the region's early period of isolation. One of these is the velvet worm, which has short, thick legs and a segmented body like a fleshy milli-pede, and which seems to be a form intermediate to annelid worms (such as earthworms and leeches) and arthropods (insects and crustaceans). In partic-ular, the rain forest has allowed the evolution of an amazing range of animals with grasping tails. As well as monkeys, porcupines, mice, rats, opossums, the fruit-eating kinkajou raccoon, and even some

FOCUS ON

BRAZILIAN COASTAL FOREST

The tropical forests of northeastern South America lie mostly within Brazil. Passion flower and bougainvillea sprawl through the trees where the marmoset lives. Pollinated by countless small birds and bats, these vines provide a lot of the monkey's food—in the form of fruit, flowers, and nectar, or the small invertebrates and insects sheltering there.

Animals in the forest rivers range from clouds of tiny biting insects to large alligators. Many river species once inhabited the ocean; these include sharks, sawfish, sole, needlefish, and rays, as well as large marine toads and the manatee. Riverine predators include the piranha fish and the caiman, which itself falls prey to the anaconda snake. Birds, such as the scarlet ibis, the spoonbill, and the hoatzin, visit the rivers to feed. Unique species include the world's only aquatic marsupial, the water opossum, and the basilisk lizard, which can run over the surface of the water.

In higher regions, few plants grow at ground level, but at low altitudes, the forest floor is barely penetrable. Most of the mammals, such as the monkeys, live up in the tree canopy. Ground-level animals include the tapir, the swamp deer, the paca, and the capybara, which is the world's largest rodent.

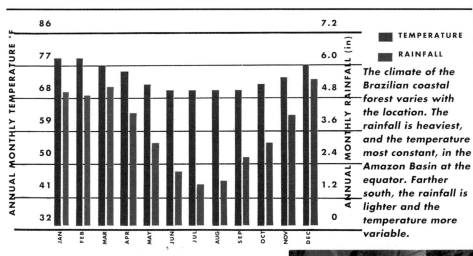

TEMPERATURE AND RAINFALL

■ TEMPERATURE
▨ RAINFALL

The climate of the Brazilian coastal forest varies with the location. The rainfall is heaviest, and the temperature most constant, in the Amazon Basin at the equator. Farther south, the rainfall is lighter and the temperature more variable.

tree snakes, have this useful "extra limb." One rea-son for this may be the frequency of flooding in large areas of rain forest at specific times of the year, forcing animals to travel from branch to branch instead of along the ground.

A wide variety of monkeys can coexist in the rain forest by feeding on different kinds of food at different levels of the forest trees. These monkeys include the callithricids, but because the tamarins and marmosets hate water, they have evolved into many different species separated by the rivers and tributaries that divide up the rain forest. ■

NEIGHBORS

Animals living in the South American forests have many neighbors— some of which, such as the pampas cat, ocelot, and jaguar, are highly dangerous to small tree-living monkeys.

OCELOT

Itself hunted mercilessly for its fur, the ocelot is an occasional predator of marmosets and tamarins.

RED HOWLER MONKEY

One of the largest New World monkeys, the red howler utters deafeningly loud calls.

Illustrations Kim Thompson

COASTAL BRAZIL

Brazil comprises almost half the land area of South America and a high proportion of the world's rain forests. Along the coast to the east of Rio de Janeiro is situated some of the fine coastal forests of the country. The area shown on the map is home to the rare golden lion tamarin.

RIO DE JANEIRO

Martyn Colbeck/Oxford Scientific Films

WOOLLY SPIDER MONKEY

Also called the muriqui, this now endangered species inhabits the forests from Bahia to São Paulo.

AGOUTI

These large but secretive rodents help to disperse the seeds of rain forest trees by feeding on fallen fruit.

FIELD MOUSE

The South American field mouse spends most of the night in trees, where it feeds from plants.

THREE-TOED SLOTH

Some sloths never leave the trees; this species descends to defecate. It eats leaves, tender shoots, and fruits.

TREE ANTEATER

Active at night, the tree anteater or tamandua climbs around with the help of its prehensile tail.

FOOD AND FEEDING

Marmosets and tamarins eat a wide range of vegetable matter, including fruits, flowers, nectar, and plant exudates (gums, saps, and latex). They rarely eat leaves, but they do eat leaf buds. They also eat frogs, snails, lizards, spiders, and insects, killing them usually with a bite to the head. The fruits they favor are usually small and sweet—figs, for example, are popular. Tamarins and marmosets spend a large part of their active time—about 25 percent—foraging for animal prey, searching through piles of fresh and dead leaves and along branches, and peering and reaching into holes and crevices in tree trunks and branches.

MARMOSETS

Marmosets are primarily fruit-eaters, with flowers, animal prey, and, especially at times of fruit shortage, exudates and nectar also being important. They never pass up a chance to eat insects that have been disturbed by swarms of army ants. The pygmy marmoset, however, feeds main-

---

THE MARMOSET'S LONG INCISORS ENABLE IT TO GOUGE TAPHOLES IN TREES TO EXTRACT SAP AND GUM

---

ly on exudates, spending up to two-thirds of its feeding time tree-gouging for gums and saps. It also eats a lot of spiders, and only rarely touches fruit.

No marmoset species share the same forest area, possibly due to their specialization on plant exudates. The common and black tufted-ear marmosets probably rely on saps and gums to supplement their diets so that they can survive the relatively harsh environments of northeast and central Brazil.

When looking for insects, it seems that marmosets and tamarins, like other predators, rely upon general features such as size, color, movement, and "configuration"

clues, such as body symmetry and the presence or absence of legs, to find their prey. Experiments with Geoffroy's tufted-ear tamarin—an insect-eater—showed that it recognized its prey of stick insects and mantids by the presence of head and legs. Stick insects normally keep their legs pressed close to their bodies; the moment one stretches a leg out, it is easily detected.

TAMARINS

Tamarins eat a range of foods similar to marmosets, but they do not eat sap, gum, or latex from trees as frequently

Color illustrations Wildlife Art Agency

A GOELDI'S *marmoset feeding on a praying mantis (below). Mantids prey on other insects, relying on their cryptic coloration and sticklike body to lure a meal within reach of their traplike forelegs.*

GREEN TREE FROG

PRAYING MANTIS

BANANAS

GIANT GRANADILLA

TREE SAP

B/W illustrations Ruth Grewcock

Jaw illustrations Elisabeth Smith

(in) SIGHT

TAMARIN JAW

canine

short incisors

long incisors

canine

MARMOSET JAW

GUM-EATERS

The pygmy marmoset and the larger marmosets have teeth that are uniquely specialized for gouging trees for gum extraction. Very little gum is actually exuded, however, and the marmoset may spend only a minute or two licking from any one hole.

Unlike the tamarins, marmosets have large incisors—almost as long as the canines—with a chisel-like structure. Marmosets anchor their lower incisors in the bark and gouge upward, producing an oval hole 1 in (2–3 cm) across. Favorite trees can be covered with larger holes and channels as long as 4–6 in (10–15 cm).

A GOLDEN-HEADED

lion tamarin eating soft fruit (left), *which provides much of its water requirements.*

Pygmy marmosets licking sap from a gouged tree hole (below) *in the upper Amazon Basin.*

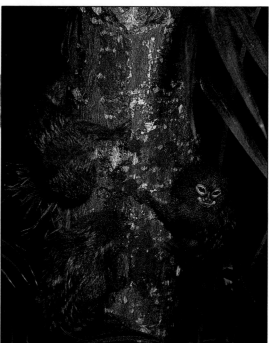

Rod Williams/Bruce Coleman Ltd.

as marmosets. They tend to lick the gum from the cuts in trees that have already been made by other animals. Some species are more restricted in their diets. For example, some black tamarins seem to eat only fruit, while on the other hand the golden lion species is an omnivore, eating both plant matter and meat. It collects fruit, flowers, gum, and nectar from around its treetop home, and also searches among the branches for insects, frogs, lizards, snails, and birds' eggs.

SHARED FEEDING SITES

Unlike marmosets, tamarin species will share the same forest areas, since they differ in their foraging habits and in the levels and exact sites at which they habitually search for animal prey (with the odd exception: see Insight page 1501). Like the marmosets, the mustached and emperor tamarins are thought to use a foliage-gleaning and visual searching method of foraging, but the lion and saddle-back tamarins are more manipulative. They search in holes or break open masses of leaf mold, rotten wood, and bark to seek out insects and their larvae. Lion tamarins have long, fine hands and fingers compared to those of other tamarins and marmosets, presumably an adaptation to this investigative style of foraging. ∎

SOCIAL STRUCTURE

Marmosets and tamarins tend to live in small family groups, numbering up to about 12 in marmoset groups, and 6–24 in tamarin species. Surprisingly, however, captive callithricids seem to live more happily in pairs with two to four offspring, so it is probable that the wild animals group together mainly for better defense against predators.

Most species seem to be strongly territorial, the females being particularly aggressive toward other groups. They mark their gouged tree holes and other landmarks with scent secretions and urine. They also make high-pitched calls, some of them inaudible to the human ear, which probably help to define a group's territory to other groups. The

> DOMINANT ANIMALS WITHIN A MARMOSET GROUP SCENT MARK MORE OFTEN THAN OTHERS, AS IF TO ASSERT THEIR POWER

black tamarin, for example, calls from an exposed branch in the early morning with a high-pitched twittering sound, and the calls are answered by nearby groups of black tamarins.

Family groups defend a home range—as little as 0.2–0.7 acres (0.1–0.3 ha) in the pygmy marmoset, up to 25–100 acres (10–40 ha) in others. The area depends on the food sources and the size of the animal. Groups visit about one-third of their range each day, traveling up to 0.6–1.2 miles (1–2 kilometers), mainly in the trees. Range defense is a lively exercise of calling, chasing, and displaying when two groups meet. Marmosets have distinct white genitalia and display their rumps with their

Michael Dick/Animals Animals/Oxford Scientific Films

COTTON-TOP
tamarins enjoying the company of the family group (above).

Geoffroy's tamarins grooming each other in the forests of northwest Columbia (left).

INTERACTIVITY

**A study has been made into why groups
from two tamarin species, the emperor
and the saddle-back, are often seen
together. Tamarins do coexist, but these
two species have a very similar diet;
why do they not avoid each other?**

**Most likely, there are subtle differences
in diet and habitat utilization so that, in
reality, they are not competing with each
other. Meanwhile, their similarities offer
benefits, with vocal exchanges providing the extra safety that comes with
numbers. Alternatively, low-level
competition may have just begun
where the two species overlap, and
eventually only one species will remain.**

tails raised and fur fluffed up. Lion tamarins
raise their manes, while tamarins fluff their
fur and tongue-flick.

Group social interaction comes to the
fore in looking after the young and mutual
grooming, most often between the adult
breeding pair and their latest offspring.
Grooming helps establish positions in the
hierarchy and may reduce stress and
calm any aggression. An adult generally
grooms its mate with its teeth and tongue,
grooming itself by scratching methodically
with its claws. Facial expressions are also
used in communication.

ADULT HELPERS

All the members of a group take an active
role in caring for the young. They carry
infants around and pass them manageable
pieces of food, such as insects. They also help
feed any individual with its hands full, such as
the breeding female or one carrying infants.
This form of assisted breeding is thought to be
unique among primates. There are benefits for
adult helpers who stay with the group, as they
can learn valuable tips for successful breeding.
During their rounds of duties, they will be waiting
for suitable breeding habitats to become available
for them. They may even get a chance to breed in
their own or a neighboring group.

Breeding callithricid monkeys have a higher
reproductive potential than any other primate: In
suitable conditions a female marmoset can produce
twins about every five months. ∎

Illustration Phillip Hood/Wildlife Art Agency

LIFE CYCLE

Marmosets, unlike many of the higher primates, have a courtship ritual. They may mate at almost any time of year, probably because the seasons vary so little in the Tropics. The male walks with his body arched, smacking his lips and flicking his tongue. He and the female groom each other, licking and using their incisors as combs. When the female is in season, the male busily scent marks objects with glands on his scrotum.

Only the dominant adult female in the group breeds during a season, although she may mate with more than one male. She keeps other females

---

ONCE PREGNANT, A FEMALE REMAINS FAITHFUL TO HER MATE: SHE WILL NEED HIS HELP IN REARING HER OFFSPRING

---

from breeding by secreting special chemicals (pheromones) from her scent glands. Gestation lasts about 20 weeks. Twin births are common with marmosets—for two-thirds of cases in the common marmoset and nine-tenths in the pygmy marmoset. Triple births are not unusual.

Most tamarins, too, seem to be nonseasonal breeders. Their courtship, however, is brief. The young are born after a gestation period of 20–21 weeks; in 80–90 percent of cases these are twins. They are close replicas of their parents, but with shorter hair and less pronounced manes. Young lion tamarins are born fully furred and with their eyes open and weigh around 2 oz (60 g). All newborn

FROM BIRTH TO DEATH

COMMON MARMOSET

GESTATION: 140–150 DAYS	**WEANING:** 4–7 WEEKS
LITTER SIZE: 1–4, USUALLY 2	**INDEPENDENCE:** 9 WEEKS
BREEDING: NO SPECIFIC TIME	**SEXUAL MATURITY:** 12–18 MONTHS
WEIGHT AT BIRTH: NOT KNOWN	
EYES OPEN: NOT KNOWN	**LONGEVITY:** NOT KNOWN
FIRST WALKING: 21 DAYS	(UP TO 10 YEARS IN CAPTIVITY)

GOLDEN LION TAMARIN

GESTATION: 126–133 DAYS	**WEANING** 4–7 WEEKS
LITTER SIZE: 1–3, USUALLY TWINS	**INDEPENDENCE:** 10–20 MONTHS
BREEDING: NO SPECIFIC TIME	**SEXUAL MATURITY:** 15 MONTHS
WEIGHT AT BIRTH: 2 oz (60 G)	**LONGEVITY:** NOT KNOWN
EYES OPEN: AT BIRTH	(10–15 YEARS IN CAPTIVITY)
FIRST WALKING: 21 DAYS	

AT 2–3 WEEKS *the youngster is starting to investigate its surroundings, but its father is never far from its side.*

THE YOUNG SUCKLE *from their mother. They start taking soft food from about four weeks.*

Illustrations Robin Budden/Wildlife Art Agency

GROWING UP

The life of a young marmoset

THE FEMALE

is receptive every two and a half weeks. She mates with one or more of the males.

THE YOUNG

are carried (below) *until six or seven weeks old.*

THE MALES

do their share of the parental duties, carrying the young when they are not being suckled.

ⓘnSIGHT

A CARING FATHER

After the birth of twins it is normally the father who plays with them, and carries them on his back for their first month or two. This helps relieve the load on the mother. When they are very small, the father sometimes carries them around his neck like a scarf. The mother may carry them too, but as a rule she tends to them only when they need to feed from her.

This caused a tragedy the first time marmosets were bred in captivity. The keepers decided to take away the male to "be on the safe side," and they removed the animal that was not carrying the young. This turned out to be the female, and it led to the young marmosets starving to death.

animals cling tightly to the mother or father. If the male is caring for the young, then every two to three hours he transfers one to the mother, passing it into her arms. She suckles the offspring for 15–30 minutes and then hands it back to the father.

When they are about three weeks old, the young start exploring their surroundings, but rush back to their parents if even slightly alarmed. At four weeks old they start taking soft food, although they

WHILE A BREEDING PAIR TENDS TO ITS YOUNG, THE REST OF THE FAMILY GROUP KEEPS A SHARP LOOKOUT FOR PREDATORS

are not yet weaned. They can survive independently at the age of two to five months, but prefer to stay with their parents, running to them if alarmed, and often begging food from them.

Marmoset litters are heavy, at 19–25 percent of the mother's weight. Helpless at birth, the newborns are carried for their first two weeks by other group members. By two months they can travel alone, catch insects or rob them from others, and spend long periods in play, chasing and tussling with one another and other group members. (This is a little earlier than young tamarins, which take about two and a half months to reach independence.) They reach puberty at 12–18 months and adult size at two years of age. The tamarins, lion tamarin, and Goeldi's monkey give birth to smaller young; in these species the male does not take charge of offspring until they reach 7–10 days old. ∎

JEWELS OF THE AMAZON

THE WORLD HAS DONE TOO LITTLE TO PROTECT THESE ENCHANTING PRIMATES—AND FOR SOME OF THEM IT MAY SIMPLY BE TOO LATE. NOW, AT LAST, EFFORTS ARE BEING MADE TO BUY THEM SOME TIME

At least one-tenth of the Amazonian rain forest has been destroyed, mainly through clearance for agriculture and tree-felling for lumber. In particular, the forest habitats of marmosets and tamarins have been greatly depleted during this century. The golden lion tamarin nearly became extinct in the wild, but a captive breeding program initiated in the 1970s has led to the reintroduction of some animals into their original environment.

The golden lion tamarin and its related subspecies are found only in a few isolated areas in the Atlantic forest region of eastern Brazil. It was here that European settlers landed over four centuries ago, and the region is now the most densely populated of all Brazil. The golden lion tamarin has

Brian Kenney/Planet Earth Pictures

Golden lion tamarins (above) *have been the subject of rescue operations since the early 1970s.*

THE SMALLEST KNOWN MONKEYS ARE FACING EXTINCTION IN FORESTS NEAR SOME OF THE WORLD'S LARGEST CITIES

always been restricted to forests of an altitude below 985 ft in coastal areas of the state of Rio de Janeiro, and possibly neighboring Espirito Santo. This type of tropical forest is easily cleared for farming and housing and stands less chance of survival than the more remote upland forests. The early 1970s saw a steep increase in deforestation in the Rio area, when a bridge connecting the city with Niterói across the bay made it considerably easier for developers to gain access to, and degrade, the last few strongholds of these tiny primates.

The golden lion tamarin's matchless beauty may be in its favor today, but it has in the past counted strongly against it. The animal has long been hunted for local use, and it has been popular as a pet since the 17th century. Hundreds of animals were exported legally in the 1960s until protective measures

came in at the end of the decade; this was followed by countless illegal exports through the early 1970s. Even today, a few individuals are trapped, mostly for the local Brazilian market.

Reports suggest, too, that local people in Rio de Janeiro have been eating lion tamarins. Often a local custom such as this one can be stopped only by informing those involved of the full impact of their activities, and presenting ideas for ways in which their natural resources could be better, and more profitably, utilized.

Like some other callithricids, the golden lion tamarin lives only in areas of primary rain forest; that is, forest that has not been affected by human intervention. It lives high in the tree canopy, but because it is sensitive to direct sunlight, it usually retreats into

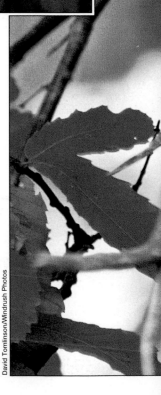

David Tomlinson/Windrush Photos

A cotton-top tamarin (right) *surveys its domain in a zoo on the Isle of Jersey.*

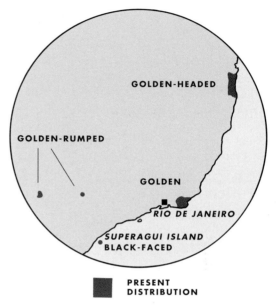

THEN & NOW

This map shows the present distribution of the wild populations of lion tamarins.

GOLDEN-HEADED

GOLDEN-RUMPED

GOLDEN

RIO DE JANEIRO

SUPERAGUI ISLAND
BLACK-FACED

PRESENT DISTRIBUTION

With at least 10 percent of the South American rain forest already destroyed, there are continuing threats to the survival of the rarest tamarins and marmosets.

The ecology of South America's forests has been developing in isolation for the last 100 million years, resulting in unique wild habitats. Unless it is done selectively, deforestation is irreversible and the benefits—temporary grazing or cropland, or timber—are far outweighed by the permanent damage caused to ecosystems.

Selective forest clearance gives the forest a sporting chance of survival, but most tamarins and marmosets need the vine thickets and continuous canopy of undisturbed forest, and the remaining stands of suitable habitat are being carved into isolated pockets. Their suffering and decline has perhaps been inevitable, in that they live in what has become the most densely populated part of Brazil. Of the original Atlantic coastal forest area—the lion tamarins's habitat—only one-fiftieth remains, the cleared land giving way to banana, cocoa, and rubber crops. Unless real progress is made in preserving the remainder of Brazil's wild places, the reintroduction of callithricids will be rendered futile.

denser foliage during the hottest part of the day. Unlike some other platyrrhine species, the golden lion tamarin will only enter and settle in undisturbed forest—of which there remains precious little.

SAVING THE GOLDEN LION

Conservationists within Brazil have been trying for years to convince both public and government of the unique importance—and desperate plight—of the callithricids. A joint conservation program set up in the 1980s involved staff from the Rio de Janeiro Primate Center, the Brazilian Forestry Development Institute, and the World Wildlife Fund–US Primate Program. This project found wild lion tamarin populations in only two areas of

> THE GOLDEN LION TAMARIN IS ALMOST ENTIRELY TREE-DWELLING AND NEEDS AN UNBROKEN CANOPY OF VIRGIN FOREST

Brazil. One was a stand of coastal forest south of the mouth of the São João River; the other was the Poço das Antas Biological Reserve established some ten years earlier, chiefly to protect this species. The first of these had been parceled up for housing developments, rendering it useless for wild monkeys. Poço das Antas represented a better opportunity for conservation, as it was already officially protected and held some 250 golden lion tamarins. It was, however, divided by road and railroads, a dam under construction was going to flood part of it, and there were too few guards to keep out the poachers. In addition, about a tenth of the reserve was mature forest and only about a third of this was suitable habitat for lion tamarins.

NEW INITIATIVES

A new program is under way, with the additional input of the Washington National Zoo. It aims to present information on the ecology of, and on changes in, the remaining lion tamarins' population in the reserve, to restore at least some of the forest habitat, and ultimately to reintroduce individuals into remote parts of the reserve. The tamarins' survival in the wild relies heavily on the outcome of this kind of environmental project. The good news is that the golden lion tamarin is doing well in captivity, particularly in the United States and Europe. From under 100 in the early 1970s, the total captive population has since risen fivefold. Specimens from Brazil have been sent to the United States to ensure genetic diversity. But the animal traffic also moves in the other direction, and tamarins bred in zoos around the world have been returned to Brazil and released in order to restore wild populations. More

Donald Nausbaum/Tony Stone Worldwide

ENDANGERED SPECIES

A DYING BREED?

The golden lion tamarin is critically endangered everywhere, mainly through loss of habitat. More recently it has bred successfully in zoos around the world, and some animals have been released into southeastern Brazilian rain forests. The wild population is currently estimated at 450, with some 560 in captivity.

The golden-headed, golden-rumped, and black-faced tamarins live in tiny areas in the states of Bahia, São Paulo, and Superagui Island respectively. They are all likewise endangered, and the techniques that have been developed to conserve the golden lion tamarin are now being applied to these species and subspecies. Work with the golden-headed tamarin has been quite fruitful, with nearly 300 already in captivity. Some breeding groups have been transferred to zoos outside Brazil, and reintroduction into the forests has started at the Una Reserve. There are thought to be around 550–600 in the wild. However, the status of the golden-rumped lion tamarin is the most desperate, with a total of only about 150 in the wild and some 65 in captivity.

The other most endangered marmoset and tamarin species are the white tufted-ear and buffy-headed marmosets and the white-footed, pied, and cotton-top tamarins. Similar conservation precautions are needed for these species too, even though their plight is not as fully realized as the well-publicized problems of the lion tamarins. Like the lion tamarins, the two marmosets are confined to the coastal forests of southeastern Brazil. They have in the past been used for biomedical research and traded as pets.

The pied tamarin lives in Brazil north of the Amazon River and appears to be reasonably adaptable and able to survive in disturbed forests,

A CAPTIVE GOLDEN LION TAMARIN (*RIGHT*). ZOO POPULATIONS NOW HAVE A ROSIER FUTURE.

CONSERVATION MEASURES

● In 1972 the plight of the golden lion tamarin first gained world attention. A meeting hosted by the Washington National Zoo was told that both wild and captive populations were decreasing. An international program was started in 1973 to scientifically manage captive groups; this has led to a healthy and growing captive population.

● In 1974 the Poço das Antas Reserve was set up. It started a reintroduction program in 1983, and

ut the continued growth of the city of
Manaus may precipitate its decline.

The white-footed tamarin is confined to a
small region in northern Colombia and,
although it seems to survive in secondary
forests, its range is now very fragmented.
is protected by law but apparently does
ot occur in any protected areas.

The cotton-top tamarin is found in forest
dges, and even secondary areas, from
osta Rica south to northwest Colombia. It
eems that it can even benefit from selective
ogging that opens up dense forest areas,
nd in some places its numbers may have
ncreased when the American Indians'
ntensive agriculture was reduced after the
rrival of European settlers. Overall,
owever, the cotton-top's population is
hrinking because of the sheer scale of
eforestation in the region.

Inset Nick Gordon/Survival Anglia

ver 70 lion tamarins have been
eleased since then. Some of these
urvive today, with new offspring.

Landowners are now setting
side forest areas for further
eintroduction projects
nvolving all callithricid species.

● In 1991 the ownership of
aptive lion tamarins was
eturned to the government
f Brazil.

MARMOSETS AND TAMARINS IN DANGER

THE FOLLOWING SPECIES ARE THREATENED TO VARYING DEGREES,
ACCORDING TO THE INTERNATIONAL UNION FOR THE
CONSERVATION OF NATURE (IUCN), OR THE WORLD
CONSERVATION UNION, RED DATA LIST, 1990:

BUFFY TUFTED-EAR MARMOSET	ENDANGERED
BUFFY-HEADED MARMOSET	
LION TAMARINS, ALL SPP.	
PIED BARE-FACED, SILVERY-BROWN	
BARE-FACED, AND COTTON-TOP TAMARINS	
GOELDI'S MONKEY	RARE
BEAR-EAR MARMOSET	VULNERABLE
TASSLE-EAR MARMOSET	
EMPEROR TAMARIN	THREATENED

ENDANGERED MEANS THAT THE ANIMAL IS IN DANGER OF
EXTINCTION AND ITS SURVIVAL IS UNLIKELY UNLESS STEPS ARE
TAKEN TO SAVE IT. THE GOLDEN-RUMPED LION TAMARIN IS
PROBABLY THE RAREST AND MOST ENDANGERED PRIMATE IN
SOUTH AMERICA.

Ken King/Planet Earth Pictures

than 70 tamarins were received by Brazil in a six-
year period up to 1990. As if the lion tamarins do not
have enough to contend with, a blaze in February
1990 destroyed more than a third of the 20 sq mile
(52 sq km) Poço das Antas Reserve. Luckily, the
tamarins live in the wooded areas, while the fire
mostly affected the brushland.

OTHER LION TAMARINS

It is much the same story for the other lion tamarin
subspecies. In 1983 it became known that up to half
of the golden-headed species' population had been
illegally removed from Brazil on behalf of Belgian
and Japanese animal traders. International pressure resulted in the return of most of them to
Brazil, where they have been used in a captive
breeding program.

The golden-rumped lion tamarin has always
been confined to the interior of São Paulo,
Brazil's most highly developed region. Much of its
habitat had already been cleared by the early
1900s, and no tamarins were seen from that time
until 1970, when a remnant population was discovered in the Morro de Diablo State Forest
Reserve in extreme southwest São Paulo. A few
years later, a smaller number was also found in
the much smaller Caitetus Reserve in central São
Paulo. These isolated populations are almost certainly the last wild survivors of this species.

The golden-headed lion tamarin's small wild
habitat range, in southern Bahia, is one of the

ALONGSIDE MAN

JERSEY SAVIORS

The Jersey Wildlife Preservation Trust on the Isle of Jersey was founded by Gerald Durrell. Through its captive breeding program it is raising lion tamarins and other rare callithricids; it has also helped to buy vital habitat in Brazil. In 1987, the Trust sent a Jersey-born pair of golden lion tamarins back to the forests in Poço das Antas, and within a year they produced twins—the world's first ever birth in the wild to captive-bred adults. In the trust's International Training Centre, students from abroad can learn how to manage rare species, before returning home to put their new skills to use in preserving local threatened wildlife.

Hulton Deutsch Collection

Irene R. Lengui/The Environmental Picture Library

Naturalist and writer Gerald Durrell (above) *is a world-renowned specialist in saving rare animals.*

A Brazilian child with his pet monkey (left). *People who live along the river often keep animals in captivity to please paying tourists.*

few parts of eastern Brazil where large forest areas remain. Even these are being felled and cleared for agricultural projects, and the area's one biological reserve was not improved by an invasion of squatters in 1980. Fortunately, however, the Rio de Janeiro Primate Center holds a colony of this and the golden-rumped species.

THREATENED CALLITHRICIDS

There are problems for other callithricids, for example in the upper Amazon region. Here, the complex systems of small, regularly flooding tributaries have, during the course of time, created many isolated colonies of the tiny, tree-bound monkeys. In consequence, several subtly different species live in a relatively small area of forest, and they are therefore highly vulnerable to habitat destruction.

Marmosets and tamarins were once—quite wrongly—thought to carry yellow fever and malaria, and they were persecuted as a result. Until the early 1970s they were exported in high numbers to zoos and for biomedical research. Today export is banned in all countries except Bolivia, Panama, and French Guiana, but it may be too late for some species. Unless the abuse of the forests is halted, the lion tamarins, the marmosets of southern and southeastern Brazil, and such species as the pied tamarin will shortly be extinct in the wild. ■

INTO THE FUTURE

The survival of the lion tamarins can be assured only by a full-scale, integrated conservation program that involves protecting the remaining natural habitat and the few surviving wild animals. Populations have, however, become so low that the species must also be bred in zoos, and these captive populations must be kept healthy by ensuring that they do not become inbred. Consequently, different breeding centers have to cooperate to arrange breeding between groups.

The golden lion tamarin now has an established captive breeding population, and a reintroduction program is now established to restock suitable areas of natural habitat with the captive-bred animals. In order for this process to be successful, the tamarins have to be carefully prepared before their release into the wild. The animals are first kept under conditions as similar as possible to those found in the forest, and once released they are monitored and

PREDICTION

COOPERATE TO SUCCEED

There is no reason why self-sufficient populations of all species should not thrive if the current conservation measures are maintained by both local and international communities.

helped with additional feeding each day until they have learned the new skills they need to survive in the forest.

Conservation of species is not cheap. The lion tamarin's reintroduction program has about 45 surviving animals, and each of these cost around $22,500 in air freight, scientists' and field assistants' wages, and a full educational program. But if the animals continue to breed well the cost per tamarin will fall steadily. The program has also developed techniques that can be used to save other rare primates, as well as preserving coastal forest to the benefit of many species.

Success depends greatly on the response of local people in the rain forest lands. They could make more money by protecting the forest than by destroying it, and the controlled harvesting of valuable natural foods such as cocoa and Brazil nuts, and drugs such as curare, could become the rain forest commerce of the future. ∎

SAVE THE NEW SPECIES!

Amazingly, a new subspecies of lion tamarin was discovered as recently as 1990 and was announced to an international meeting on lion tamarin conservation in June that year. Christened the black-faced lion tamarin, the new species was found on Superagui Island about 155 miles (250 km) south of the massive Brazilian city of São Paulo.

The new discovery has a golden-colored body with a black face, hands, and tail—more or less a reverse of the golden-headed subspecies. It seems that local fishermen had been reporting its presence for some years, but few people believed the stories.

When Brazilian biologists Maria Lucia Lorini and Vanessa Persson finally went to investigate, they found that the rumors were true; although, sadly, their first sighting was of a black-faced tamarin lying dead in the road. With the further help of the local fishermen, they then found a small group of the monkeys living in a forested area. They have since estimated that there may be a total population of 200 animals, to be found only on this small island.

As a result, soon after its discovery, an International Recovery Committee was formed to safeguard the new subspecies. Unfortunately, the black-faced lion tamarins live in a part of Superagui Island that is not set aside as a national park. Pressure is being applied on the authorities to get the park boundaries redefined in order to give this rare tamarin better protection—an essential move if this beleaguered subspecies is to survive into the next century.

Illustration Steve Kingston

OPOSSUMS

John Shaw/NHPA

THE WORLD'S FIRST POUCH

INFINITELY VERSATILE AND ADAPTABLE, AMERICAN OPOSSUMS ARE AMONG THE OLDEST MARSUPIALS KNOWN: THEIR ANCIENT ANCESTORS TROD THE SOIL ALONGSIDE THE DINOSAURS

I n 1520 the Spanish Royal Court received Vincente Pinzón, a navigator who had known the New World since the days of Columbus. The voyager beckoned King Ferdinand and Queen Isabella to stroke the animal in his hands. Their royal fingers found a small pouch on the animal's abdomen. Inside was a group of thimble-sized, suckling young.

In this way Europeans saw their first marsupial, a southern opossum. Of the nine marsupial families, the most dramatic are surely the kangaroos and wallabies, but the opossums of North and South America, all part of the family Didelphidae (di-DEL-fid-ie), are distinctive for different reasons. The only marsupials living outside Australia and its neighboring islands, they also provide a direct link with the earliest mammals. Fossil evidence indicates that the first mammals, living more than 65 million years ago, closely resembled the modern Virginia opossum.

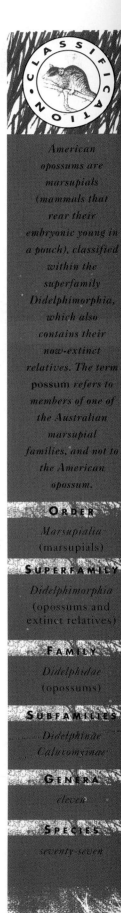

1511

Woolly opossums are highly specialized. They feed on fruit and nectar in tropical American forests.

The wide range of the opossums—found from southern Canada to the tip of Patagonia—confirms their reputation as survivors. They are at home in deciduous woodlands, Andean highlands, jungle riverbanks, and even suburbs. Some opossum species have evolved to thrive within a single habitat, while others are more versatile, coping with wide extremes of climate and landscape.

The smallest opossum, of the genus *Marmosa*, is mouse-sized, and its newborn offspring are barely larger than grains of rice. The largest, the Virginia opossum, is the size of a small dog.

THE WORD *OPOSSUM* COMES FROM VIRGINIA ALGONQUIN WORDS MEANING "WHITE DOG"

Despite their range of size and habitat, most opossums share certain characteristics such as a long, pointed skull; small ears; and a tail that is prehensile (able to grasp). There are five toes on each foot, and one toe on each hind foot is opposable, like a human thumb. The tail and toe features are useful to the many tree-dwelling opossum species. Opossums are omnivorous. Their fifty teeth contain many incisors as well as fanglike canines. Plant-eating kangaroos, by comparison, have only thirty-two teeth and no canines.

The differences between species are fascinating examples of adaptation. The yapok, an aquatic

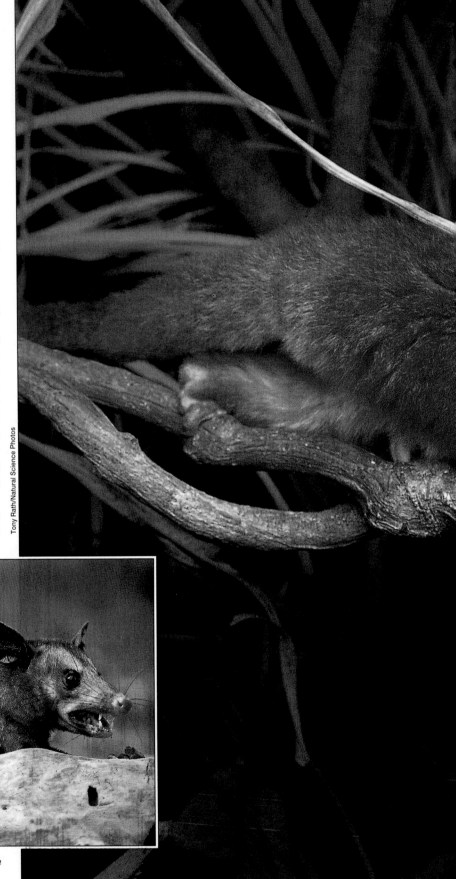

Tony Rath/Natural Science Photos

Daniel Heuclin/NHPA

The southern opossum (above) of Central and South America is equally at home in grassland or forest.

Beady, buttonlike eyes and a white face are distinct features of the Virginia opossum (below).

Brian Kenney/Planet Earth Pictures

species, has webbed feet and sleek fur like that of an otter. The mother can use a sphincter muscle to shut the pouch while she swims, leaving her young dry and able to continue suckling. Short-tailed opossums live mainly on the ground and have much smaller tails than the tree-dwelling species.

Perhaps the most interesting point of variety is in the pouch. Some pouches open to the front, others to the back. The rat-tailed opossum has lateral skin folds instead of a full pouch. The little water opossum has no pouch at all, and the young must cling to a nipple or grasp the mother's fur.

Opossums date back to the late Cretaceous period, 65–90 million years ago, when North and South America were still joined. Fossils from that time show that among the earliest mammals were

MISCONCEPTIONS

As the only marsupials in the Americas—coupled with the fact that they are nocturnal, so little was known about them—opossums were the victim of folktales. It was once thought that they mated through their noses and that the young were later blown into the pouch.

This false belief probably arose when tiny opossum offspring were noticed in a mother's pouch shortly after she had investigated it with her nose. Also, females often lick the pouch area before giving birth.

marsupials resembling Virginia opossums. The link is the jawbone. The Cretaceous mammals, like the modern Virginia opossum, had five upper incisors and four lower ones. The sharp molars indicate that these mammals, like opossums, had a wide-ranging diet that included meat.

North and South America drifted apart about 65 million years ago. Fossil remains of opossum-like mammals also stop in North America at this time; the marsupials there probably lost out to placental mammals. There are probably a number of variables that gave placental mammals the competitive edge.

The South American marsupials were luckier. With less competition from placental mammals, they evolved into a wide variety of species, many of which crossed the land bridges that still connected South America with Antarctica and Australia.

Australian marsupials flourished in isolation once Australia split away from other landmasses. South American marsupials fared less well. Most species died out after North and South America reconnected two or three million years ago, ushering in a wide range of placental mammals.

Opossums were the exception. They continued to diversify and still thrived in South America. The Virginia opossum, North America's only marsupial, even went against the flow of mammal traffic, crossing the isthmus of Panama and recolonizing North America. Even now it is expanding its range northward and westward. ■

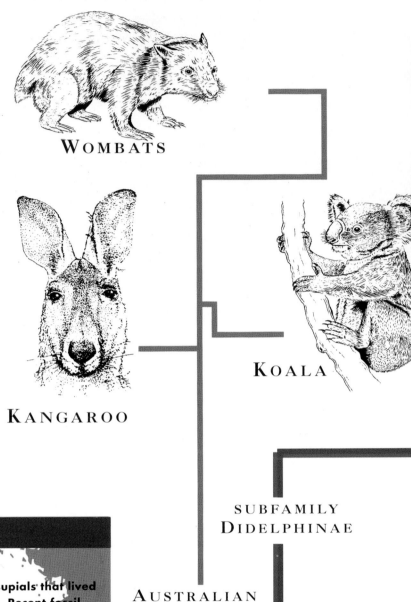

WOMBATS

KANGAROO

KOALA

SUBFAMILY
DIDELPHINAE

AUSTRALIAN
MARSUPIALS

AMERICAN
OPOSSUMS
(DIDELPHIDAE)

MARSUPIALS

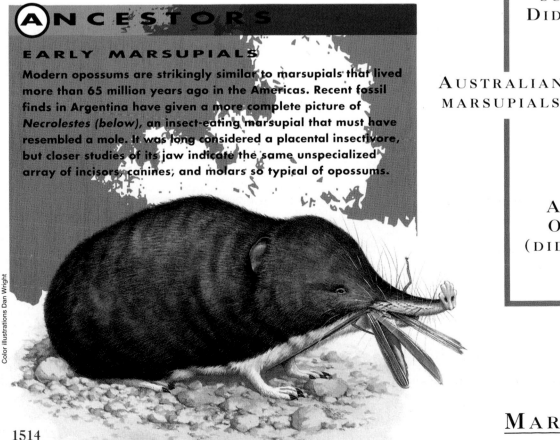

ⒶNCESTORS

EARLY MARSUPIALS

Modern opossums are strikingly similar to marsupials that lived more than 65 million years ago in the Americas. Recent fossil finds in Argentina have given a more complete picture of *Necrolestes (below)*, an insect-eating marsupial that must have resembled a mole. It was long considered a placental insectivore, but closer studies of its jaw indicate the same unspecialized array of incisors, canines, and molars so typical of opossums.

Color illustrations Dan Wright

THE OPOSSUMS' FAMILY TREE

The Didelphid family of American opossums comprises two subfamilies. There are eight genera and about seventy species in the Didelphinae (di-DEL-fin-ie). The three genera and five species of Caluromyinae (kal-yoo-ro-MIE-in-ie) opossums range from Central America through northern South America.

OTHER SPECIES:
"FOUR-EYED" OPOSSUM
MOUSE OPOSSUM
SHORT-TAILED OPOSSUM
SOUTHERN OPOSSUM
THICK-TAILED OPOSSUM
WHITE-EARED OPOSSUM
YAPOK (WATER OPOSSUM)

VIRGINIA OPOSSUM
Didelphis virginiana
(di-DEL-fis ver-jin-ee-AH-na)

The Virginia opossum is the only marsupial species native to the United States. It is the largest and most wide-ranging of all the **opossums and takes its name from the state in which it was first closely studied in the 17th century. It is highly adaptable and** **can cope readily with sudden changes to its environment, including widespread human settlement.**

WOOLLY OPOSSUM
Caluromys lanatus
(kal-yoo-RO-mis la-NAH-tus)

There are three species of woolly opossums, which take their name from their soft fur. These tree-dwelling opossums all have long prehensile tails, which are longer than the head and body combined. Pictured at right is the Ecuadorean woolly opossum.

SUBFAMILY
CALUROMYINAE

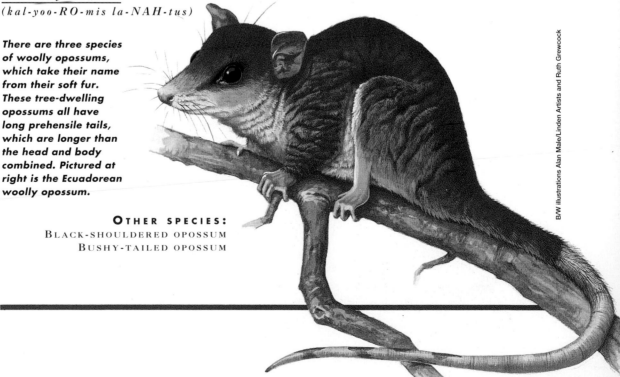

OTHER SPECIES:
BLACK-SHOULDERED OPOSSUM
BUSHY-TAILED OPOSSUM

B/W illustrations Alan Male/Linden Artists and Ruth Grewcock

ANATOMY:
THE OPOSSUM

Opossums range in size from the mouse opossum (above left), with a head-and-body length of 2.7 in (6.8 cm), to the Virginia opossum (above right), which has a head-and-body length of 13–22 in (33–54 cm).

HEARING

is the opossum's most acute sense, and the thin, hairless ears are usually moving. Many Virginia opossums at the northern extremes of their range lose their ear flaps to frostbite.

THE EYES

protrude and are specially adapted to help the opossum see better during its twilight and nighttime hours of activity.

VIRGINIA OPOSSUM POUCH

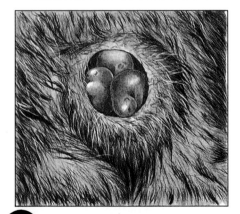

YAPOK POUCH

POUCHES

There is a great deal of variety in pouch shape among species, and some simply have lateral skin folds or no pouch at all. The Virginia opossum pouch (far left) is fully formed and faces forward. The backward-facing yapok pouch (left) can be shut tight with the sphincter muscle.

SKELETON

The long, prehensile tail and clawed, five-digit feet enable the Virginia opossum and other arboreal relatives to climb easily and to remain secure on branches. The Virginia opossum has a cat-sized body but is heavier and has shorter legs.

OPOSSUM SKELETON

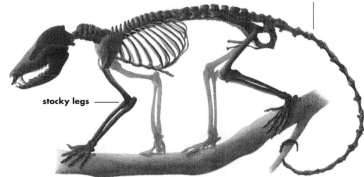

prehensile tail

stocky legs

SKULL

The facial part of the opossum's skull, which is long and pointed, coupled with a narrow cranial part give an overall effect of elongation. There is a pronounced ridge—the sagittal crest—along the top of the cranium. The jaws are flexible enough to remain open at right angles for up to fifteen minutes.

X-ray illustrations Elisabeth Smith

OPOSSUM TRACKS

There are five fully developed toes on all four feet, although tracks made by the hind feet are easily recognizable because of the opposable "big toe."

HIND FOOT

FOREFOOT

THE FUR

varies among species, from smooth in mouse opossums to woolly in woolly opossums. Some genera, such as the Virginia opossum, have long, projecting guard hairs.

THE HIND LEGS

are longer than the forelegs in adults, although newborn opossums have well-developed forelegs to pull them to the mother's pouch.

HE CLAWS

re sharp to help in grasping or climbing. hey grow on all digits except the pposable large toe on each hind foot.

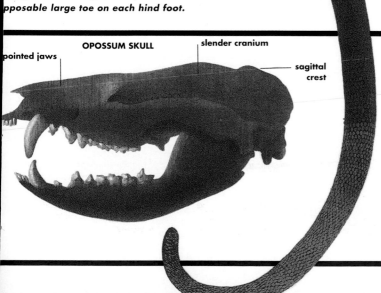

OPOSSUM SKULL   slender cranium

pointed jaws

sagittal crest

TEETH

Opossums have fifty teeth, more than any other marsupial. They have many incisors in both the upper and lower jaws, as well as long canines and sharp molars. This arrangement favors an omnivorous diet.

several incisors

long canines

sharp molars

Main illustrations Barry Croucher/Wildlife Art Agency

CLASSIFICATION

GENUS: *DIDELPHIS*
SPECIES: *VIRGINIANA*

SIZE

HEAD–BODY LENGTH: 13–22 IN (33–54 CM)
TAIL LENGTH: 10–22 IN (25–54 CM)
HEIGHT: 7–10 IN (16–25 CM)
WEIGHT: 4.4–13.2 LB (2–6 KG)
WEIGHT AT BIRTH: 0.007 OZ (0.2 G)

COLORATION

VARIES FROM ALMOST BLACK THROUGH MOTTLED TO CREAMY YELLOW. FACE AND SNOUT ALWAYS WHITE, REGARDLESS OF BODY COLOR

FEATURES

DISTINCT, REAR-FACING POUCH
LONG PREHENSILE TAIL
LONG, NARROW MUZZLE
SHORT LIMBS, WITH HIND LIMBS LONGER THAN FORELIMBS
OPPOSABLE LARGE TOE

THE TAIL

of an opossum is frequently longer than the body, and the base is enlarged to store fat in some species. The tail, often prehensile, is either naked or only partially covered in fur.

Afraid of No Human

Opossums are nocturnal and solitary animals. They are also opportunistic and resilient, which probably accounts for their survival over the last sixty-five million years

Some opossums inhabit burrows dug by other animals, and they will even share living spaces with armadillos or other animals. Smaller tropical species, such as mouse opossums, build nests in banana stalks. Occasionally mouse opossum families have arrived in Europe or North America with a consignment of bananas. Usually, though, nests are in some sort of dark haven, often no more than a hollow tree trunk or rocky crevice.

The opossum makes the nest more comfortable with a layer of leaves and grass, and its method for carrying these building materials to the nest is striking. The opossum picks up the leaves or grass with its mouth and then passes them between its forelegs. Its long, hairless tail folds forward under the body to hold the materials in place. In this way, an opossum can load as many as eight mouthfuls before returning to the nest.

Safe in its nest, the opossum sleeps most of the day, with its hairless ears folded. Breeding pairs will share a nest, well away from other opossums. Except for breeding, opossums derive no advantages from contact with others of their species.

Night Rambler

At dusk the opossum begins the search for food. It will peer around with its bulging eyes, pointing its long snout this way and that. But sight and smell are much less important than hearing. An opossum is acutely sensitive to sound—be it the footfall of a human or dog or the distinctive slither of a worm that might become its next meal. The naked ears are constantly moving, twitching in response to the slightest sound.

A single male will make an area of woodland his own, staking his claim with saliva deposits for the benefit of other opossums. Territories can overlap, however, with up to 260 opossums sharing a square mile (100 per square kilometer). Opossums will peacefully gather at a common food source, but in more difficult conditions a chance meeting of two males usually results in a dispute. The standoff begins with both males opening their mouths wide, displaying their fifty teeth. It then escalates into a series of hisses, growls, and loud screeches. Having made their case, both opossums usually move off.

Defensive Ploys

A cornered opossum will sometimes threaten an intruder in a similar way. It can open its mouth wide—as much as ninety degrees—displaying its teeth for up to fifteen minutes. Even the tiniest opossum species will use this tactic. A group of unattended young mouse opossums, no bigger than beetles, will meet an aggressor with gaping, hissing mouths.

Mouse opossums (above) *are tiny, but they will hiss fiercely at predators, just like their larger cousins.*

SOUNDS OF SILENCE

Opossums, like most marsupials, are much quieter than placental mammals. But their narrow range of vocalization ties in with their solitary and nomadic lifestyle. They have no real need to communicate with other opossums except in disputes over territory or while breeding.

In disputes with other opossums, and when trying to scare off predators, opossums employ a range of hisses, growls, and shrieks. While breeding and at certain other times, opossums emit a distinctive metallic clicking sound from their lips. Young opossums that have fallen from the pouch emit an ultrasonic cry that is inaudible to humans.

Playing possum, or feigning death, is usually a response to a predator such as a dog or fox. Oddly, this tactic seems to work, and the bemused attacker often moves on (see page 1528).

AN UNLIKELY TAIL

Opossums' distinctive body features play a role in their behavior. The long prehensile tail has many functions besides carrying twigs. It is particularly useful in trees, where many opossums spend much of their time. The opossum can wrap its tail around a branch, but for most species it serves more as a brake or fifth climbing hand than as an anchor. Unlike spider monkeys, for example, fully grown opossums cannot hang by their tails for long periods.

There is a popular misconception that a mother opossum extends her tail forward over her back so that her young can use their tails to "lock" themselves on for a secure ride. Opossums have never been observed to do this; however, in the past, wishful artists have depicted them in such a position. There have even been photographs of opossums in this position—but these were staged, using stuffed museum specimens.

The yapok has a wider, flatter tail. This South American opossum is mainly aquatic and climbs very little. The tail helps it swim. Mouse opossums, inhabiting a range of dry regions of South America, also have wide tails, but theirs are full of fatty deposits—good nourishment when there is little available food. ∎

Young southern opossums are adept at piling onto their mother's back to hitch a handy ride.

HABITATS

Opossums are infinitely adaptable: They inhabit great swaths of North America and nearly all of South America, except for the highest Andes. The ability to thrive in such diverse surroundings is remarkable, particularly when compared with the marsupials of Australia. There, humans have become a serious threat and many marsupials have been forced back to small centers of their ranges or into sanctuaries. By contrast, many opossum species have dramatically widened their ranges since the arrival of large-scale human settlement.

GENERALIZED OR SPECIALIZED

Besides the official classification, opossums can be divided into two general groups depending on their habitat. Generalized species, such as the Virginia and southern opossums, are the real survivors, adapting to the widest range of climate and landscape. Specialized opossums have adapted to particular conditions, such as highlands or tropical riverbanks, where they flourish. These latter opossums are more threatened by humans because they occupy fragile environmental niches.

The Virginia opossum is the most familiar and widespread species, ranging from southeastern

in SIGHT

"SHREW" OPOSSUMS

Seven species of "shrew" opossums live in the wet, cold cloud forests of the highest Andes. These opossums are only about 8 in (20 cm) long, half of which is tail. Fossils indicate that the "shrew" opossums, with no pouch and only a few incisors, diverged from the family tree even before the Australian marsupials did. They are now classed in their own family, Caenolestidae (kie-no-LEST-id-ie).

The "shrew" opossum lives chiefly on the ground, using its long tail mainly as a balance as it bounds along well-marked trails in the undergrowth. It prefers mossy slopes and ledges protected from winds and cold rain. The "shrew" opossum feeds mainly on insects, earthworms, and other small invertebrates.

Canada and the eastern United States all the way south to the River Plate in Argentina. It has been introduced, and thrives, in scattered pockets along North America's Pacific coast.

Opossums generally favor forested or brushy areas, although they also live in more open country as long as there are wooded waterways nearby. The Virginia opossum prefers moist woodlands or thickets near swamps and streams. That type of

Woolly opossums (below) live in trees in the equatorial forests of America. They are highly agile, searching the branches for fruit, leaves, and live prey.

DISTRIBUTION

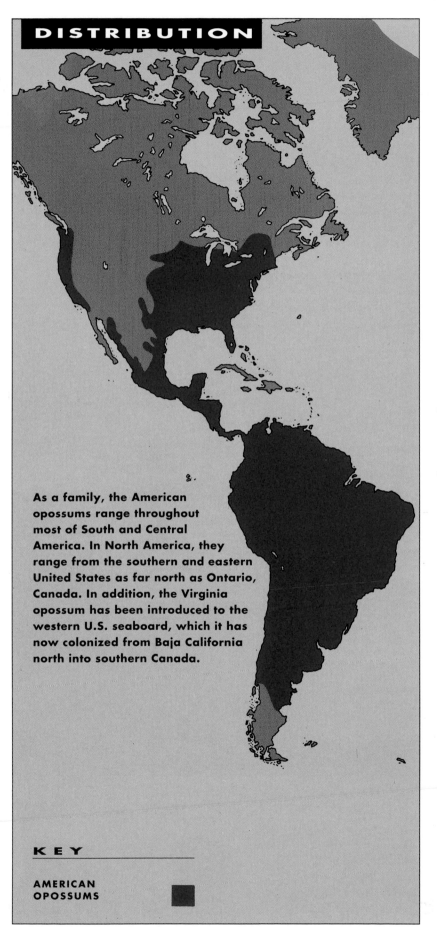

As a family, the American opossums range throughout most of South and Central America. In North America, they range from the southern and eastern United States as far north as Ontario, Canada. In addition, the Virginia opossum has been introduced to the western U.S. seaboard, which it has now colonized from Baja California north into southern Canada.

KEY

AMERICAN OPOSSUMS ■

landscape is common in Virginia, where the species was first studied closely.

THE GREAT COLONIST

Virginia, apart from lending its name to the common opossum, also marked the northern edge of the opossum's territory when the first settlers arrived in North America in the 1600s. The opossum has steadily spread north and west since that time. After being introduced to a pocket of California in 1890, the opossum went on to occupy the whole U.S. Pacific Coast and into southwestern Canada. It is estimated that in the last fifty years alone, the Virginia opossum has extended its range by more than 800,000 sq mi (2,000,000 sq km).

This expansion is almost certainly a result of the opossum's ability to coexist with humans. Despite being trapped for their pelts and eaten as a delicacy in the South, opossums have matched the westward expansion of American settlers almost step for step. Garbage cans, dumps, farms, and poultry houses have become traditional food sources.

IT MAY BE THAT THE VIRGINIA OPOSSUM'S RANGE EXPANSION WAS AIDED BY HUMANS, WHO KILLED OFF MANY OF ITS PREDATORS

In southeastern Canada—the northern limits of the Virginia opossum—winter temperatures commonly fall to –22°F (–30°C). Deciduous trees have largely yielded to pines at this latitude, and snow covers the ground for more than five months a year. It is here that the opossum's resilience is stretched to breaking point, with ears and tail falling victim to frostbite. Yet conditions well within its established range can be nearly as hostile. Consequently, it could be argued that the sparseness of the human population, rather than the harshness of the climate, dictates the opossum's northern limit.

OPOSSUMS IN SOUTH AMERICA

The southern opossum is equally at home with humans; it has been seen nesting in trees along some of the busiest city streets in South America. The southern opossum's territorial range and pattern of behavior in the wild resemble that of the Virginia opossum. These opossums seem most prolific in moist broad-leaved forests of tropical and semitropical South America.

The Andes host a number of South American opossums. Five species of shrew opossums live in the high forests and meadows of the Andes; they thrive in altitudes of up to 13,200 ft (4,000 m). They prefer cool, damp, densely vegetated areas and use runways along surface vegetation to go from one feeding territory to another.

The "shrew" opossums share their Andean range with some of the forty-six species of mouse, or murine, opossums. These distinctive opossums have prominent eyes that reflect light as a deep ruby red. In some species the tail is twice as long as the rest of the body. As a result, most mouse opossums live in trees, using their strong, prehensile tails to anchor themselves when feeding. Other mouse opossums make their homes in Mexican cacti or in the banana plantations of Central America.

Many opossum species inhabit the tropical lowlands east of the Andes. The woolly opossum, southern opossum, and Virginia opossum are generalized species that range throughout the region. Other opossums, such as the tree-dwelling ashy murine opossum and the aquatic yapok, focus on one aspect of this rain forest. Abundant food makes this region densely populated with opossums, but different species coexist with little competition.

The thick-tailed opossum is well suited to the vast, grassy pampas of South America. Its hairy tail does not grip well and the "thumb" on each foot is not fully opposable; but these shortcomings do not trouble it in a land of so few trees. Thick-tailed opossums are also less solitary than other species.

Erwin & Peggy Bauer/Bruce Coleman Ltd.

FOCUS ON

WEST VIRGINIA

West Virginia is one of the northernmost of the "southern" states in the United States. The Allegheny mountains, part of North America's Appalachian Range, cover two-thirds of the state. Slopes, many of which exceed 4,000 ft (1,250 m), are heavily wooded. Forests cover 62 percent of West Virginia, yet the state's human population is less than two million. The forest cover is mixed, with oaks and maples sharing space with hardwood nut trees such as hickory and walnut. Peach, apple, and cherry trees grow well in West Virginia, and fruit cultivation is the main farming activity in cleared land.

The climate is humid, with the Atlantic influence slightly modifying the continental extremes. These conditions, which encourage a profusion of wildlife, particularly favor the Virginia opossum. Its arboreal, nocturnal lifestyle is well suited to the forested landscape, while fruit orchards provide rich pickings in times when animal prey is hard to find.

Once considered Virginia's "poor relation" because its land is less arable, West Virginia is now promoting itself as a wilderness playground. Opossums, although occasionally the victims of hunters, thrive on the scraps left by human interlopers.

TEMPERATURE AND RAINFALL

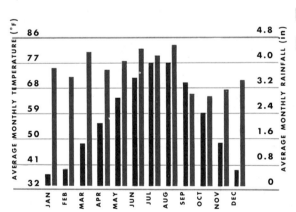

■ TEMPERATURE

■ RAINFALL

The data here apply to West Virginia's capital, Charleston; the Appalachians have a similar, but slightly cooler and drier, climate. Temperatures and rainfall peak during the summer, but most months see appreciable rainfall.

The Patagonian opossum lives farther south than any other marsupial. The landscape near the extreme tip of South America is nearly treeless, so this opossum has become a ground-dwelling predator. Its toes are stronger and more pronounced than those of other species, making it easier to scamper along the grassy pampas. As in some other species, its tail thickens with fatty deposits at certain times of the year as a reserve for lean times. Its short, broad skull and long canine teeth suit its role as a hunter of small birds and mice. ■

NEIGHBORS

In the forests and uplands of West Virginia, the black bear and eagle are potential threats to opossums, while raccoons and squirrels often compete with them for food.

AMERICAN BLACK BEAR

The black bear is the largest carnivore of the Appalachians, measuring up to 5 ft (1.5 m) long.

AMERICAN BEAVER

The amphibious beaver is easily recognized by its long, sharp incisors and broad, flat tail.

Illustrations Joanne Cowne

WEST VIRGINIA

The Appalachian Range forms most of the border between West Virginia and Virginia. Most of the state's unspoiled forests and wildlife are in this Appalachian area. The mighty Ohio River, which forms most of the state's western border, also marks the beginning of the rich farmlands of the U.S. Midwest region.

OHIO
Ohio River
WEST VIRGINIA
KENTUCKY
VIRGINIA
TENNESSEE
NORTH CAROLINA

STRIPED SKUNK

Armed with its repellent scent glands, the striped skunk is a fearless denizen of the American forests.

BALD EAGLE

The bald, or American, eagle is a large, fish-eating raptor and the national bird of the United States.

BULLFROG

The largest of all North American frogs, this species is named for its size and its deep voice.

GRAY SQUIRREL

Always alert, the gray squirrel seems poised for escape, even when stuffing its mouth with nuts.

BLACK WIDOW

One of the few poisonous spiders of North America, the female is jet-black with distinctive red markings.

FOOD AND FEEDING

Opossums are omnivores—they can eat just about anything. This ability to select a wide-ranging diet has helped them survive competition from other mammals, changes in landscape and climate, as well as the arrival of humans.

The key to this feeding flexibility is the opossum's jaw, and more specifically its teeth. Its set of fifty teeth features very serviceable canines and incisors. A wide-open jaw flashing these pointed tools is a useful deterrent, but the dental arrangement also means that the opossum can take its pick of carrion, insects, small vertebrates, mushrooms, fruit, berries, or grain.

Opossums are free to concentrate on any of these food sources if they are plentiful. Some localized species even feed almost exclusively as carnivores, herbivores, or insectivores because of limits imposed by habitat or their own adaptations. The more widely distributed species, such as the Virginia opossum, are more opportunistic. They are also more likely to view human settlements as a source of food.

A MOUSE OPOSSUM IN MEXICO WAS SEEN HANGING IN A FIG TREE BY ITS TAIL, HOLDING THE FRUIT IN ITS FOREPAWS

In its forest habitat, a Virginia opossum will use its acute hearing to detect its prey. The slightest sound, such as a crunched leaf or breaking twig, will cause the opossum to start. In the summer, it might begin its nocturnal feeding by listening for faint rustlings caused by earthworms, snails, grasshoppers, or toads. If lucky, it might startle a mouse, vole, small bird, or snake.

The opossum is always willing to stop and nibble fruits and berries, even when there is ample prey at hand. Animal food sources become scarcer in late autumn and winter, so the opossum turns to plants. Persimmons and pokeberries, which are both common in the American South, are particular favorites. Observers of "bloodthirsty" opossums in thickets have usually been misled by the purple pokeberry juice dribbling from the animal's snout. Extra winter nourishment, from either animal or plant sources, is essential in the northern range of the Virginia opossum. This builds up a store of fat to carry it through its periods of relative inactivity.

The southern opossum is often seen as a counterpart of the Virginia opossum. Its feeding pattern closely resembles that of the Virginia opossum, alternately hunting and gathering to exploit food sources. An individual southern opossum's feeding range varies over the course of a year, becoming slightly larger during the rainy season.

The gray and black "four-eyed" opossums of Central and South America are also omnivorous and opportunistic. Their name—"four-eyed"—refers to a white spot above each eye, giving them a disconcerting appearance when viewed head-on.

Living as far north as Canada, the Virginia opossum must struggle through long winters. Prey is scarce during these cold months, but the opossum simply adjusts its diet to plant matter. This adult (below) is drinking from the snow-fed waters of a stream.

K. Maslowski/Frank Lane Picture Agency

FOOD

Virginia opossums eat a varied diet, depending on territory, time of year, and other factors. They prefer to eat insects and other small vertebrates but will also dine on a variety of plants.

GRASSHOPPER

POKEBERRY

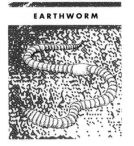

EARTHWORM

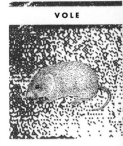

VOLE

Illustrations Ruth Grewcock

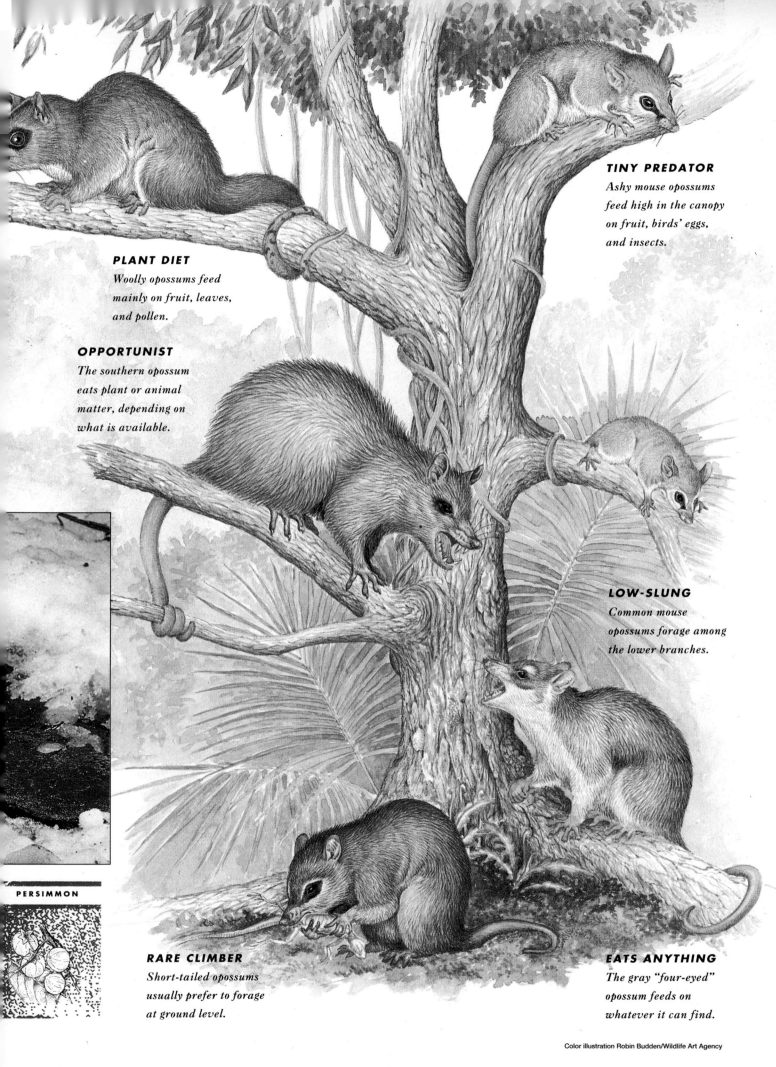

PLANT DIET
Woolly opossums feed
mainly on fruit, leaves,
and pollen.

OPPORTUNIST
The southern opossum
eats plant or animal
matter, depending on
what is available.

TINY PREDATOR
Ashy mouse opossums
feed high in the canopy
on fruit, birds' eggs,
and insects.

LOW-SLUNG
Common mouse
opossums forage among
the lower branches.

PERSIMMON

RARE CLIMBER
Short-tailed opossums
usually prefer to forage
at ground level.

EATS ANYTHING
The gray "four-eyed"
opossum feeds on
whatever it can find.

Color illustration Robin Budden/Wildlife Art Agency

1525

Marty Stouffer/Oxford Scientific Films

A Virginia opossum (above) *maneuvers cautiously in a persimmon tree to bring fruit within its grasp.*

Like the Virginia opossum, they eat small mammals, reptiles and their eggs, birds, insects, fruit, and carrion. These opossums are sometimes blamed for serious damage to orchards and cornfields. They are more active during the day than most opossums.

RIVER MARSUPIAL

The more specialized opossums are fruit-eaters, although some are carnivorous. The water opossum, or yapok, is an otterlike species that feeds on frogs, crayfish, shrimp, and fish. It swims well with its webbed hind feet and thick tail, leaving its unwebbed forefeet free to grab prey.

The first skin of a yapok was sent to Europe nearly two hundred years ago. At first naturalists thought it was a type of pygmy otter because of its dense, waterproof fur and webbed feet. A later examination of a skull indicated that it was in fact an opossum. Not even in Australia, where marsupials evolved into counterparts of mice, badgers,

and wolves, had any taken to an aquatic lifestyle, and the yapok is unique in this respect. It has been observed holding a small fish in one hand and eating it from end to end until it is finished. The yapok has a wide range, from southern Mexico to northern Argentina, but is not common anywhere.

Woolly opossums, members of the smaller Caluromyinae subfamily, are among the most specialized of all opossums. Most of their adaptations suit their flying-trapeze–like existence in the highest reaches of tropical forests. Woolly opossums are much more agile than most didelphids, thanks to their long, flexible tails, which act as balances on

*in*SIGHT

CALLING ON RESERVES

Many opossum species are able to remain dormant in a nest for a number of days when food sources are scarce. This period of lethargy is similar to hibernation, with decreases in body temperature, breathing rate, and heartbeat slowing down the body's metabolic rate. During this time the opossum uses fat deposits that have been stored under the skin, often at the base of the tail. Compared to true hibernation, however, this lethargic state can be controlled easily and lasts for only a few days. Also, it is more of a response to hunger than to cold. For example, it can occur during long periods of dry weather.

An Alston's mouse opossum in Costa Rica (above) *devours its luckless prey—a katydid.*

WATER OPOSSUM

The yapok (left) *lives an aquatic lifestyle in the tropical freshwater streams of America. An able swimmer, it preys on amphibians, crustaceans, and fish.*

the slender upper branches. Keen eyesight also plays a part in their feeding success, climbing among branches in search of fruit, leaves, and small insects. In the dry season they feed on the nectar of flowering trees and even act as pollinators.

FIERCE MICE

Mouse opossums have earned a reputation as fierce fighters and will often kill and eat rodents as large as themselves. One mouse opossum species, *Murina robinsoni*, lives the life of a nomadic hunter. As well as feeding on a typical range of rodents, lizards, and birds' eggs, it dispatches large grasshoppers with a series of bites to the head and thorax. Feeding seems more important than nesting for this opossum, which simply crawls into the nearest dark shelter when daylight arrives.

Opossums find nourishment in sometimes forbidding habitats, but in the food-rich tropical forests they also show a remarkable ability to coexist with each other. As many as seven species can share territory in these forests; there is surprisingly little competition, largely because they specialize in finding food at different forest "altitudes." The ashy mouse opossum and woolly opossum might inhabit the rain forest canopy, with the common mouse opossum on lower branches. Gray "four-eyed" and southern opossums would range between lower branches and the ground, with various short-tailed opossums remaining on the ground. ■

Illustration Sean Milne

1527

TERRITORY

Opossums tend to avoid each other's company except when breeding. A territory contains important sources of food and shelter, and most opossum communication involves warning off rival males or unwanted suitors. "Four-eyed" and short-tailed males, for example, often broadcast their presence in an area by marking twigs and other points along their way with saliva.

WANDERING AT WILL

But opossums show few of the elaborate claim-staking measures taken by territorial mammals such as otters or even domestic cats. Radio-tracking studies of the Virginia opossum have shown it to be locally nomadic, without defended territories. Like other opossums, it has a home territory, but this often overlaps with those of the same species.

This home range varies among species and even with individual opossums. Much of the movement within the range is between nest and feeding sites, so the territory will expand or shrink according to available food supplies or breeding factors. Male home ranges overlap greatly, and each usually overlaps several female ranges. Females occupy exclusive home ranges for at least part of the year.

Mainly carnivorous species, such as the Virginia and southern opossums, usually occupy larger territories than the more specialized fruit-eating species. The average Virginia opossum

PLAYING POSSUM

To play possum is an expression meaning "to play dead" and refers to the opossum's ability to feign death. It uses this defensive tactic when threatened by a predator. The opossum lies on its side with its tail and body curled and its mouth open, and it remains in this state for many hours. The baffled predator usually abandons the opossum, which then escapes. It seems that certain predators that avoid carrion, such as dogs, are confused and believe that the opossum is dead.

No one is quite sure how this tactic works. It may be similar to fainting in humans, but some studies, using brain scans, found that "playing possum" is just that—playing—and that the animal's brain was functioning in a normal, alert state.

S. Maslowski/Frank Lane Picture Agency

abandon ranges where predators such as wolves, bobcats, and owls are active. Faced with threats within its own territory, the opossum will hiss, growl, and bare its many teeth, but it often adopts the more passive defense tactic of playing possum.

WELCOME HANDOUTS

An obvious territorial influence is the presence of humans. Opossums will often adjust their territorial ranges to benefit from garbage cans, poultry runs, orchards, and other food sources. The opossum's territory, in the widest sense, has expanded alongside that of humans.

home range is 50 acres (20 hectares), while that of a woolly opossum is only 0.75–2.5 acres (0.3–1 hectare). With their lack of territoriality, opossums do not patrol the whole home range on a regular basis. A Virginia opossum's nightly travel of about 1.2 miles (two kilometers) would consist almost exclusively of foraging. Territorial marking would not play any part in this patrol.

In many respects, opossums define their territories in relation to other species. The Virginia opossum might widen its range to compete with other mammal species with similar feeding patterns, such as raccoons and lynx. Likewise it will constrict or

AMAZONIANS

The black-shouldered opossum lives in the Amazon in Peru, where its partially naked tail helps it grip the branches of trees in the humid rain forest.

SOME FEMALE MOUSE OPOSSUMS ARE HIGHLY INTOLERANT OF ONE ANOTHER, KEEPING STRICTLY SEPARATE TERRITORIES

Some opossum species take this territorial link with humans further. One species of short-tailed opossum, *Monodelphis domestica*, gets its name from its "domesticated" habit of living in Brazilian houses. There the territories of the opossum and the humans coincide to the advantage of each. The opossum gets a wide range of nesting sites, such as under floorboards, and a varied diet of scraps. The humans benefit from the opossum's skill at dispatching rodents, insects, and scorpions. ■

Illustrations John Morris/Wildlife Art Agency

TINY PREDATORS

"Shrew" opossums scuttle along runways through dense undergrowth, only rarely taking to the trees.

LIFE CYCLE

Opossums live only for about two years, so they must take bold steps to propagate the species—and as their 65-million-year history shows, their success rate is high. Most opossums have some sort of pouch for the young, but even the pouchless species give birth to tiny, helpless offspring. Most development takes place during lactation, when all nourishment comes from the mother's milk.

Breeding is timed so that the young will leave the pouch when food resources are most plentiful. Most tropical species, as a result, can breed at any time, while those in temperate or montane habitats have specific seasons. Opossums in the seasonal tropics breed so that the young will emerge at the start of the rainy season. Virginia opossums usually breed twice a year, in January or February and then again about 110 days later. In their warmer southern range they might have a third litter, while in the north there is sometimes just one.

There are no elaborate courtship rituals or long-term bonds. If a male meets a female during the breeding season, the initial aggressive displays of hissing and teeth-baring quickly give way to courtship. The male initiates proceedings by approaching the female while making distinctive, metallic vocal clicks. If the female is in estrus, she will allow the male to mount her. Copulation may last as long as six hours.

Gestation is remarkably short—only twelve to thirteen days. The female gives birth in her nest to as many as twenty-five offspring, which are born in a space of about five minutes. These tiny pink babies look more like worms than mammals. They do, however, have claws on their forefeet to help them climb the 3 in (8 cm) from the birth canal to the pouch. The claws then drop off.

More than half of these young might die on the way to the pouch, and the number of nipples inside defines the upper limit of litter size. Virginia opossums have thirteen nipples arranged in a circle with one central nipple, but there are usually about seven young in a litter. Most other species have smaller litters, averaging about four.

The young are in effect "feeding machines" at this stage. They cannot yet regulate their body heat, but the mother's pouch keeps them warm. Another feature enables them to feed almost continuously. The passage from the nasal chamber to the larynx is so separated from the esophagus that the young can breathe and feed simultaneously. The aquatic female yapok has a pouch that shuts tightly while she swims, trapping sufficient oxygen for the young prior to submersion.

Kenneth W. Fink/Ardea

COURTSHIP

The male approaches the female (above) *while making clicking noises. If she is not in estrus, she remains aggressive, and the male will eventually give up and go away. If she is in estrus, copulation will follow.*

CARE OF THE YOUNG

Seen from a human perspective, opossums display a curious mixture of ruthlessness and generosity in their care of the young. A litter containing only one offspring will fail because the single mouth is not enough to stimulate the mammary glands. And a Virginia opossum mother will not respond to distress calls of detached infants until they have left the pouch for good.

But Virginia opossums have been known to carry other females' young, and female pale-bellied mouse opossums will retrieve the distressed young of another female. Less is known about the possible parental-care function of the male's pouch in some species, such as the yapok.

GROWING UP
The life of a Virginia opossum

TINY YOUNG

After a gestation of twelve to thirteen days, several young are born in rapid succession. They use their foreclaws to crawl to the pouch.

EASY RIDERS

After about seventy days in the pouch, the young are finally ready to leave it. They soon get the hang of riding on the mother's back. The young will themselves breed within a year.

Life can be very trying for the female Virginia opossum, especially once her pouch is no longer large enough to house her litter of dependent young (left).

LIFELINE

Once the young reach the pouch, they sieze a nipple and hang on for fifty days. If there are more babies born than available nipples, the surplus of the litter will simply starve.

The young begin to release their grip on the nipples at about fifty days and first leave the pouch briefly about three weeks later. At first they crawl around on the mother or stay in the nest while she forages. The pouch soon becomes too small for the young, although they have not yet been weaned. During that interim they follow the mother while she forages, sometimes riding on her back.

Pouchless opossums develop in similar fashion. When the mother moves, the young are kept in a "bundle" between her hind legs or on her back.

Opossums are fully independent at three to four months old, and sexually mature two to three months later. They soon breed, because they have only about two years of reproductive activity. ∎

FROM BIRTH TO DEATH

VIRGINIA OPOSSUM	SHORT-TAILED OPOSSUM
GESTATION: 12–13 DAYS	**GESTATION:** ABOUT 2 WEEKS
LITTER SIZE: 5–25	**LITTER SIZE:** 5–12
BREEDING: FEBRUARY AND JUNE	**BREEDING:** AT ANY TIME (UP TO 4 BROODS ANNUALLY)
WEIGHT AT BIRTH: 0.007 oz (0.2 G)	**WEIGHT AT BIRTH:** 0.004 oz (0.1 G)
EYES OPEN: 3–4 WEEKS	**EYES OPEN:** 10–15 DAYS
WEANING: 12 WEEKS	**WEANING:** 7 WEEKS
FORAGING: 3–4 MONTHS	**FORAGING:** 7–8 WEEKS
SEXUAL MATURITY: 6–10 MONTHS	**SEXUAL MATURITY:** 4–5 MONTHS
LONGEVITY: 2–3 YEARS (UP TO 8 IN CAPTIVITY)	**LONGEVITY:** 2–3 YEARS

MARCHING TO VICTORY

THE VIRGINIA OPOSSUM POSSESSES A RARE DISTINCTION AMONG MARSUPIALS: ITS RANGE HAS INCREASED BEYOND BELIEF. UNFORTUNATELY, HOWEVER, ITS SOUTH AMERICAN RELATIVES ARE IN DEEP TROUBLE

 possums are something of an evolutionary success story, continuing to flourish when other marsupials were driven to extinction and holding fast in the face of human development. Generalized species, such as the Virginia and southern opossums, have even extended their ranges dramatically. More specialized opossums, however, depend on delicately balanced ecosystems, and therefore on humankind's willingness to preserve them.

RAPID REPRODUCTION

One obvious reason for the opossum's overall success is its fecundity. Even in the harshest climate, a female Virginia opossum produces at least one litter of about six young each year. Elsewhere, there can be two or three litters annually.

The opossum's birthrate and short life span make it a textbook example of r-selection. This is the ecological term used to describe a pattern of breeding and survival in a potentially unstable environment. Animals using successful r-selection breed early and often, producing large litters to ensure that at least some of the offspring survive. The opossum's life span is short, with only two years of breeding available. But during that time a mother might have between four and six litters. A conservative estimate of three surviving offspring per litter would mean that she will have been responsible for twelve to eighteen more opossums.

DIETARY ADVANTAGE

It seems that opossums have also been served by their lack of specialization. Although able to adapt to specific conditions, opossums can quickly adjust to new environments. For example, the wide range of teeth, which never evolved into one particular function, gives them a diverse choice of food sources.

The Virginia opossum's balanced diet means that it can cope with competition from carnivores such as raccoons and lynx. It has held its own—and even spread—in parts of the eastern United States where these mammals have had to retreat. The first opossums were noted as recently as the 1900s in parts of Massachusetts and Vermont, the normal haunts of more advanced carnivores. Opossums since then have flourished, while the lynx has become a rarity.

Jany Sauvanet/Oxford Scientific Films

Woolly opossums (above) *are fairly common, but they cannot match the success of their Virginia cousin.*

Robert Carr/Bruce Coleman Ltd.

THEN & NOW

This map shows how the Virginia opossum has increased its range north through the United States and Canada over the last two centuries.

///// **PRE-1800 DISTRIBUTION**

■ **CURRENT DISTRIBUTION**

Having entered North America millions of years ago, the Virginia opossum has been steadily spreading northward. In the 1600s its northern limit was Virginia. Its progress accelerated with human settlement, and by the 19th century it was reported in Canada. It is estimated that the Virginia opossum has widened its range by more than 800,000 sq miles (2,000,000 sq km) in the last fifty years alone.

The Virginia opossum's success at holding its own in more traditional habitats is equally impressive. Opossum fur is still in demand, particularly in December and January when its coat is thickest. It is estimated that more than a million opossums are trapped each year in Texas alone. Despite this trade in fur, Virginia opossum populations in such strongholds are steady and probably rising.

Apart from the Virginia opossum's opportunistic and sometimes scavenging eating habits, there is a powerful and simple reason why it has thrived near settlements: Humans kill many of its natural enemies. Opossums face constant threats from owls and foxes, but larger predators, such as wolves, bears, and bobcats, have been killed because of the threat they pose to poultry and cattle.

The Virginia opossum is extending its range even today, thriving on the by-products of civilization.

Other factors work in the opossum's favor. One might link with the old view that an opossum's odor made it unappetizing. It was claimed, quite unjustly, that the dreadful smell of the opossum would penetrate through wood and stones and would "even make anyone fall down dead."

Americans with a taste for "possum and taters" (sweet potatoes) might have dismissed this insult, but it might have held a grain of truth. It seems that opossums do not taste good to other animals.

> **SOME SPECIES OF MOUSE OPOSSUMS ARE KNOWN FROM SINGLE SIGHTINGS; THERE MAY BE OTHERS YET TO BE DISCOVERED**

Opossum remains are rarely found in foxes' dens. A dog, having killed an opossum, will shake it and then abandon it, whereas it will partially eat and then bury the remains of a woodchuck.

"Playing possum," the response to some serious threats, is another mysterious factor in the opossum's favor. Naturalists admire this ability to force a predator to beat a bemused retreat, even if they do not fully understand why it works.

Other survival qualities are more easily understood. The opossum's state of near lethargy in severe cold or drought approaches hibernation, but leaves the opossum free to reassess food prospects after a few days. It survives the loss of part of its tail and ears through frostbite. Opossum bones also seem to heal very well. Studies of opossum skeletons reveal a high number of well-healed broken

Haraldo Palo/NHPA

Thick-tailed opossums are native to South America.

bones, which other mammals of similar size would not have survived.

It is harder to judge the success of the more localized species in the Amazon rain forest and in the high Andes. Their remote habitats and nocturnal behavior limit accurate observation and population counts. Certain species and subspecies of mouse opossum, for example, were only identified in the 1980s, which leads to speculation about how many species might already be threatened by development under way in South America.

These opossums would be ill equipped to cope with sudden changes caused by tree clearance or air and water pollution. Data are not available on the effect of the decreasing ozone layer on ecosystems in the high Andes.

Brazil has long been seen as the key to both the problems facing Amazonian wildlife and to any successful resolution of these problems. Amazonia, the huge, forested area of the Amazon Basin, lies mainly in Brazil. For decades Brazilian governments have been under domestic pressure to open up more of this land to development. The political pressure, coupled with corrupting financial enticements, allowed unfettered clearance of trees, threatening the most important tropical habitats of opossums and other wildlife. ■

ALONGSIDE MAN

MISUNDERSTOOD MARSUPIALS

Opossums have endured mixed fortunes since they were first presented to Spanish royalty in the early 16th century. They were often the object of misleading information about breeding patterns and mysterious odors. The Germans even have a word meaning "marsupial stupidity," based on observation of captive opossums. Since these nocturnal creatures were being forced to live a diurnal existence in captivity, it is not surprising that they were considered stupid.

Opossum meat is a specialty of the American South, where "possum and taters" has been a rural dish for several hundred years. There is even a photograph of President Franklin Roosevelt, the epitome of Yankee values, digging in to a plate of possum alongside his beaming Southern hosts. The yapok, woolly opossum, and other species are also trapped for their fur, although not on the scale of Virginia opossum trapping. Some woolly opossum species have also been used in medical research.

INTO THE FUTURE

At first glance the opossum's future looks rosy. Using the Virginia opossum's success as a yardstick, many people might conclude that other species have thrived in their relations with humans and increased their territorial range accordingly.

But such a "special relationship" with humans does not exist for opossums in Central and South America. Many of these species exist far from human habitation and are highly specialized to their habitats. The ecosystems that support these opossums, ranging from cloud forests of the Andes to humid tropical lowlands, are delicately balanced and practically irreplaceable. The Chilean "shrew" opossum is found only in Llanquihie Province in the moist forests of southern Chile and on a small Pacific island. This opossum was only discovered when the logging industry set up in Llanquihie, and it remains to be seen whether this rare species will

PREDICTION

SPOTLIGHT ON THE AMAZON

The Amazon is a treasure to all nations, so international conservation measures are a wise move. Without a conservation plan, many of the Amazon's wildlife species will disappear before they are discovered.

survive such a wholesale change to its habitat.

There are signs of cautious optimism that Brazil might have slowed, if not stopped, the destruction of tropical moist forests in Amazonia. The Brazilian government unveiled a comprehensive environmental program for the Amazon region in 1989, following global environmental protests about the destruction of Amazonia.

But trouble lies ahead even for the Virginia opossum. Human populations in the southwestern United States are increasing rapidly, while many eastern states lose population. Many areas of the northeast are becoming reforested, and some of the original large predators are also returning. Opossums could once rely on humans to exterminate deadly enemies such as timber wolves and bobcats, but today humans see these predators in a more sympathetic light. That might be bad news for the Virginia opossum—but, then again, opossums watched as even fiercer predators, the dinosaurs, marched to extinction 65 million years ago. ■

TROPICAL SPECIES

Each year more than 32,000 square miles (80,000 sq km) of rain forest are lost—an area about the size of Maine. The forests of Brazil's Amazon Basin are the largest single element of this mass destruction, which has threatened Earth's supply of oxygen as well as many species of South American flora and fauna.

Opossums are among the threatened species, although lack of proper studies up to now means that we cannot be sure how close some are to extinction, or indeed whether currently unclassified species are being lost. Several species of mouse opossums are known from only one or two locations, while other species such as the yapok are widespread overall but scarce in any one area. It is hard to predict the effects of deforestation on dispersed species now in high numbers, such as woolly opossums and gray and black "four-eyed" opossums.

RIO DECLARATION

Brazil hosted delegates from 178 countries at the United Nations Conference on Environment and Development, or Earth Summit, June 3–14, 1992. The Earth Summit highlighted the fundamental problem facing opossums and other wildlife of the rain forests. Poorer countries such as Brazil assert the right to exploit their forest resources, and they expect wealthier countries to pay the bill if development is to be done in an environmentally friendly way.

Illustration.Joanne Cowne

INDEX

Published by Marshall Cavendish Corporation
99 White Plains Road
Tarrytown, New York 10591-9001

© Marshall Cavendish Corporation, 1997
© Marshall Cavendish Ltd, 1994

The material in this series was first published in the English language by Marshall Cavendish Limited, of 119 Wardour Street, London W1V 3TD, England.

Library of Congress Cataloging-in-Publication Data

Encyclopedia of mammals.
p. cm.
Includes index.
ISBN 0-7614-0575-5 (set)   ISBN 0-7614-0585-2 (v. 10)

Summary: Detailed articles cover the history, anatomy, feeding habits, social structure, reproduction, territory, and current status of ninety-five mammals around the world.
1. Mammals—Encyclopedias, Juvenile. [1. Mammals—Encyclopedias.] I. Marshall Cavendish Corporation.
QL706.2.E54 1996
599'.003—dc20   96-17736
                                                        CIP
                                                        AC

Printed in Malaysia
Bound in U.S.A.